Domination, Migration and Non-Citizens

Does the concept of domination cast new light on issues that arise in the context of migration and citizenship? If citizenship is a status that provides protection from domination, understood as subjection to arbitrary interference, are non-citizens – whether outside or inside the state – necessarily subject to domination by virtue of being non-citizens? Does domination provide a useful basis for considering the harms that migrants suffer? If non-domination is a value to be promoted in politics, what are the implications for the treatment of migrants and resident non-citizens?

This book addresses issues of migration and citizenship within the frame of freedom, in terms of domination, understood as being subject to the threat of arbitrary interference. Coming from a variety of perspectives, the chapters examine the issues of migration controls, differential resident statuses, including temporary workers, refugees and long-term residents, and the conditions for access to citizenship in the light of these concerns.

This book was published as a special issue of the *Critical Review of International Social and Political Philosophy*.

Iseult Honohan is Senior Lecturer in the School of Politics and International Relations, University College Dublin, Ireland. Her research interests lie in republican political theory and its applications, especially to the areas of diversity, migration and citizenship, on which she has published *Civic republicanism* (Routledge, 2002), two edited volumes, and a number of articles.

Marit Hovdal-Moan is a postdoctoral research fellow at the Philosophy Department, Norwegian University of Science and Technology, Norway. Her research focuses primarily on normative approaches to international migration management, and the moral justifiability of state borders and boundaries.

Domination, Migration and Non-Citizens

Edited by
Iseult Honohan and Marit Hovdal-Moan

Routledge
Taylor & Francis Group
LONDON AND NEW YORK

First published 2015
by Routledge
2 Park Square, Milton Park, Abingdon, Oxon, OX14 4RN, UK

and by Routledge
711 Third Avenue, New York, NY 10017, USA

Routledge is an imprint of the Taylor & Francis Group, an informa business

British Library Cataloguing in Publication Data
A catalogue record for this book is available from the British Library

ISBN 13: 978-0-415-74780-6

Typeset in Times New Roman
by RefineCatch Limited, Bungay, Suffolk

Publisher's Note
The publisher accepts responsibility for any inconsistencies that may have arisen during the conversion of this book from journal articles to book chapters, namely the possible inclusion of journal terminology.

Contents

Citation Information

The chapters in this book were originally published in the *Critical Review of International Social and Political Philosophy*, volume 17, issue 1 (January 2014). When citing this material, please use the original page numbering for each article, as follows:

Chapter 1
Introduction: Domination, migration and non-citizens
Iseult Honohan and Marit Hovdal-Moan
Critical Review of International Social and Political Philosophy, volume 17, issue 1 (January 2014) pp. 1–9

Chapter 2
Non-domination and the ethics of migration
Sarah Fine
Critical Review of International Social and Political Philosophy, volume 17, issue 1 (January 2014) pp. 10–30

Chapter 3
Domination and migration: an alternative approach to the legitimacy of migration controls
Iseult Honohan
Critical Review of International Social and Political Philosophy, volume 17, issue 1 (January 2014) pp. 31–48

Chapter 4
The problem of denizenship: a non-domination framework
Meghan Benton
Critical Review of International Social and Political Philosophy, volume 17, issue 1 (January 2014) pp. 49–69

Chapter 5
Unequal residence statuses and the ideal of non-domination
Marit Hovdal-Moan
Critical Review of International Social and Political Philosophy, volume 17, issue 1 (January 2014) pp. 70–89

Chapter 6
Republicanism and the constitution of migrant statuses
David Owen
Critical Review of International Social and Political Philosophy, volume 17, issue 1 (January 2014) pp. 90–110

Chapter 7
Immigration, interpersonal trust and national culture
Lubomira Radoilska
Critical Review of International Social and Political Philosophy, volume 17, issue 1 (January 2014) pp. 111–128

Chapter 8
Competing methods of territorial control, migration and justice
Christopher Bertram
Critical Review of International Social and Political Philosophy, volume 17, issue 1 (January 2014) pp. 129–143

Please direct any queries you may have about the citations to clsuk.permissions@cengage.com

Introduction: Domination, migration and non-citizens

Iseult Honohan[a] and Marit Hovdal-Moan[b]

[a]*Politics and International Relations, University College Dublin, Dublin, Ireland;*
[b]*Philosophy, Norwegian University of Science and Technology, Trondheim, Norway*

In Europe and other regions of the world public debate concerning how many immigrants should be admitted, which rights those admitted should have, and which conditions can be required for access to citizenship is intense and enduring, and these have increasingly become central electoral issues. On the one hand, the harsh treatment of migrants is often a matter of public criticism; on the other hand, states are concerned about problems of welfare, security and social unrest that they have come to associate with large-scale migration. At its most fundamental level, this debate concerns the question of how best to balance particularist principles of democratic self-determination and state sovereignty and universalist principles of individual freedom and human rights.

The articles in this special issue examine whether the concept of domination can cast a distinctive light on the normative issues arising in this tension between state sovereignty and universal principles with respect to migration and the position of non-citizens in contemporary liberal democratic states. These issues arise both externally insofar as foreigners are subject to migration controls, and internally insofar as migrants live in states of which they are not full members. The issue thus examines the potential of domination as a concept to bring to bear on issues of migration controls, differential residence statuses and access to membership.

In the recent elaboration of neo-republican political theory, articulated notably by Philip Pettit and Quentin Skinner, domination is defined in terms of subjection to the threat of arbitrary interference (Pettit 1997, 2012, Skinner 1998, 2008). The corresponding notion of freedom is broader than the negative conception of freedom, and requires not just the absence of interference, but protection against the threat of arbitrary interference. This account of freedom, broadly derived from the republican tradition, is understood to require certain kinds of institutional structures that guarantee the equal status of citizens, and protect them from arbitrary or discretionary exercises of power. The status of *citizenship* is thus central to the idea of freedom as non-domination, which is realized only in the context of certain political and legal structures that secure people from vulnerability to arbitrary interference.

While this account of domination has achieved considerable attention, the concept and how it is best articulated is still a matter of contention. While domination is defined in terms of subjection to the threat of arbitrary interference, the 'arbitrariness' of power may be understood in different ways. Pettit initially defined it in terms of the unchecked exercise of the dominator's will, and a failure to track the interests of the person subject to that power. But these procedural and substantive elements may be found independently. So, in refining the concept, Pettit has continued to modify the terms in which the threat of arbitrary power is formulated, to constitute a lack of 'discursive control', according to which the exercise of social power is arbitrary unless it tracks the affected parties' interests through deliberative procedures (Pettit 2001, p. 140). Frank Lovett has further refined an account of domination, while emphasizing that this is not a specifically neo-republican account. There are two important dimensions to this account. First, dependence, measured in terms of the costs of exit from a relationship, is an essential condition for domination. Second, in contrast to Pettit's substantive interpretation, on this procedural account, domination rests centrally in the potential exercise of social power according to the will or pleasure of a person or group when it is not externally and effectively constrained (Lovett 2010, p. 112). Thus, the significance of democratic citizenship as the status necessary to realize non-domination is relaxed on this account, as what matters to obtain non-domination on this account is that social power is constrained by effective rules known to all parties concerned (Lovett 2010, p. 116).[1]

The concept of non-domination has also been subject to criticism, which includes denying its independence from negative freedom (Carter 1999, 2008, Kramer 2003, 2008), questioning the relative importance of the kind of freedom identified (Markell 2008), and querying the determinacy of its policy implications (McMahon 2005).

One way of examining the strength of a theoretical construct is to examine its implications in practice. Thus, we may be able to see more clearly whether the theory of non-domination has implications for political and social life that are different from other theoretical accounts by applying it in certain critical areas. Although up to now the idea of non-domination has been articulated mainly at the domestic level and with respect to citizens of a bounded state, it springs to mind easily as having potential relevance across borders and for non-citizens in the contemporary world at a time when political theory has increasingly come to address issues of justice and freedom across borders and at a global level (Bohman 2007, 2013, Laborde 2010). Migration is one area of transnational relations in which the theory of non-domination may seem to have particular promise for application. As noted by Iseult Honohan in this issue:

> While the classic cases of domination most frequently cited are slaves and wives within a patriarchal marriage, some of the starkest contemporary examples of vulnerability to arbitrary power may be seen in the realm of migration and access to citizenship, where states are considered to have a general right to determine entry and exclusion, and where broad discretionary procedures remain particularly widespread in practice. Those who are not fully protected by the legal structures, or are not participants in the political structures, of a state may be particularly vulnerable to the threat of domination. Non-citizens are vulnerable to domination by individuals and groups in society insofar as they lack the full range of protections of citizens, and by the state insofar as they lack the power to contest its decisions politically, and insofar as its powers over them are more discretionary than over citizens.
>
> (Honohan, 2014, p. 32)

The articles here address issues of migration and citizenship within this frame of domination, understood as subjection to the threat of arbitrary interference, to explore further whether domination theory can usefully address the question of the claims of migrants in an international order where democratic self-determination and state sovereignty are prevailing principles. Does the threat of arbitrary interference affect migrants within states and extend across borders? If it does, and if migrants are thus a category that is heuristically understood as subject to domination, whom should we see as dominated: all potential migrants, including those seeking to enter, or only those who are temporary residents and permanent denizens? If non-domination is a value to be promoted in politics, and if it can address domination of non-citizens, what are the implications for the treatment of would-be immigrants, and various kinds of resident non-citizens?

The articles examine the issues of migration controls, differential resident statuses (ranging from undocumented migrants, temporary workers and refugees to long-term residents), and the conditions for recognition as citizens from a variety of perspectives. It should be noted that although the contemporary theory of domination has been closely connected with republican theory, it does not have to be understood exclusively in republican terms. Of the authors in this issue, some connect it more explicitly with republican theory than others. Likewise some address more directly the problem of defining domination precisely, and others focus mainly on its application. In any case, the focus in this issue is more to explore the implications of the concept in a new area of application than to address internal debates or external criticism of the concept itself. Sarah Fine may be seen as expressing the approach of the authors more widely, when she states in the opening article:

> The argument presented here is not intended as a critical intervention in the ongoing philosophical debate about the concept of liberty, nor is it a contribution to internal republican disputes about how best to understand the concepts of domination or arbitrariness, for example, or about the exact relationship between contemporary republican theory and its neo-Roman antecedents. [...] Rather, the main aim is to reflect upon the ethics of migration through the lens of the neo-Roman conception of political liberty, in order to see what we might learn

> both about enduring questions in the ethics of migration and about the appeal of contemporary republicanism as a political theory.
>
> (Fine, 2014, pp. 13–14).

That said, it may be noted that most authors broadly follow the concept of domination elaborated by Pettit, and several draw on the emphasis on dependence on a relationship and on the significance of external checks on social power, as articulated by Lovett. Thus, some authors adopt a version of Pettit's democratic account of substantive arbitrariness, where social power is understood as arbitrary when it does not track the interests of the affected parties through deliberative procedures, while others draw on Lovett's procedural understanding of arbitrariness, as subjection to social power unconstrained by external rules. All the authors, however, understand domination as something that can only take place in social relationships, excluding the possibility of domination without agents, that is, of social structures, systems or ideologies themselves subjecting persons or groups to domination. When applying domination to migration, several of the articles deal both with migration controls on entry, and with the treatment of resident migrants, while some focus mainly on one of these areas.

Fine opens the issue, giving a broad perspective on the potential of non-domination to illuminate the ethical issues that arise with respect to migration and access to citizenship. This is elaborated in an historically rooted account of what she cites as the twin republican principles that freedom is achieved only by the *free person* in a *free state*. She argues that the neo-republican approach seems to have most to offer when the threat of domination is immediate and clear, and when the issue of *status* is central. In such cases the type of status itself represents a clear imbalance of power, and affects the migrant's ability to live as a free person; the solutions that can be brought to bear should clearly connect the status of free person and the status of free state.

Thus, she argues that domination theory has clear implications in relation to policies with respect to refugees, stateless persons and some resident non-citizens, but faces dilemmas when it comes to international rights to free movement, where putting any limitation on the state's right to determine its members may be seen as undermining the power of the state to protect its citizens from domination – as a 'free state'.

Control over borders has long been seen as the right of sovereign states. Yet migration controls have been criticized from justice perspectives as reinforcing global distributional inequalities, and from freedom perspectives as breaching the principle of non-interference and as violating autonomy (e.g. Carens 1987, Abizadeh 2008).

Iseult Honohan focuses specifically on migration controls from the perspective of freedom from domination. She examines whether this account of freedom offers a distinctive criterion for assessing the justifiability of particular migration controls as well as of the general right of states to exclude.

She argues that understanding the infringement of freedom by migration controls in terms of domination leads to different implications from arguments based on rights of freedom of movement, or on the need for coercion to be justified by democratic legitimation. She concludes that while not all are equally dominated by migration controls, domination is exercised through such controls of a kind and an extent sufficient to warrant limits on the absolute right of states to control migration – in terms of a guaranteed status, oversight by a higher authority and rights to contest migration decisions. She argues that such limitations on the state's control of entry or membership do not essentially undermine the conditions necessary for a free state to promote non-domination.

The next three articles, by Meghan Benton, Marit Hovdal-Moan and David Owen, address the domination of resident non-citizens, and examine the justifiability of distinct forms and degrees of exclusion in liberal democratic states that affect them. Boundaries of citizenship do not coincide with territorial borders, and it appears that it is not in the interests of liberal democratic states to make them do so. The benefits of international migration make it essential for states to have flexible residency rules that allow people to enter and participate in many of the social and economic aspects of the state, without being or immediately becoming citizens. Modern liberal states thus have significant numbers of immigrants residing within their borders who are not full political members. Moreover, it may seem that the very idea of a coherent and unified political community is threatened unless there is some formal distinction between these residents and full citizens.

Benton and Hovdal-Moan consider differences in the degrees of domination of different categories of resident, and the corresponding levels of protection needed, with respect in particular to the issue of their dependence, how this changes over time, and its implications for access to rights that are often associated with citizenship. They grapple with the intuition that it is not necessarily dominating under all circumstances to be a non-citizen resident – for instance, in the case of wealthy skilled migrants, who have significant exit options and can call on diplomatic protection by their state of origin. These do not necessarily have a strong claim for immediate access to citizenship or to rights and protections exactly comparable to those of citizens.

Benton argues that although the status of being a non-citizen or 'denizen' has been described as second-class citizenship, many instances of denizenship are not morally troubling, e.g. highly skilled temporary workers who will soon return home. She develops a framework for addressing the problem of denizenship, which is structured around the ideal of non-domination. Although denizens – like citizens – are subject to the coercive power of the state, they lack many of the accountability mechanisms citizens enjoy, such as political representation. Drawing on Lovett's idea of dependence, she argues that the extent to which this differential matters for different groups of migrants is a function of their dependence on unaccountable power. This is measured in terms of the exit costs of leaving the state of denizenship: either by leaving the country or by becoming a citizen. This is not a simple linear process as the costs of exit from the state may increase over time, but the costs of exit into citizenship may decrease. She concludes by showing how this model can inform policies in three areas: making states more accountable to their non-citizen population, empowering denizens in their private relationships, and reducing arbitrariness in the process of citizenship acquisition. She concludes that our intuition that denizenship is not intrinsically dominating must be matched by scrutiny of the dependence involved in different statuses held by non-citizens.

Hovdal-Moan begins by arguing that neither an approach to migration based on equality nor one based on a rights theory is able to accommodate both the exclusive, membership dimension and the universalist, inclusive dimension of liberal democratic citizenship. Like Benton, she applies Lovett's account of domination and its focus on dependence, and argues that a concern to reduce domination will provide for stages of inclusion, or a stairway to citizenship. On the one hand, certain rights must be granted immediately to protect migrants from the acute domination that can be experienced in the areas of, e.g. employment and housing. But it does not require immediate access to political rights. Only as migrants become more enmeshed in a variety of other relationships that structure their life chances does it require their access to the political rights that allow them to participate in shaping the character of the state. Thus, this approach allows stages of inclusion (not a complete equality of status from the start). But it excludes long-term exclusion on nationalist grounds of identity. This approach, she claims, fits better with our intuitions about citizenship and with the multilayered conception of citizenship emerging in international and constitutional legal practice.

As with the two previous authors, Owen allows for different degrees of protection from domination in a state. But this article emphasizes protection not only from domination that occurs in virtue of one's status, but also from the domination occurring in the constitution of status regimes such as migration and citizenship laws insofar as these assign to all humans a particular civic status as citizen, stateless person, asylum-seeker, refugee, temporary worker or permanent resident. Thus, he considers republican conditions of legitimacy for constituting the civic statuses of migrants. He identifies two different levels of legitimacy tests to which any civic status is subject, namely: first, that it should not make its bearers more vulnerable to the arbitrary exercise of private or public power; and second, that the very constitution of the person as bearer of this status should not itself be the product of an arbitrary exercise of public power. Owen argues that the first condition significantly constrains the range of legitimate migrant statuses less secure than citizenship. The second goes further, requiring that those subject to the status regime should have an effective power to shape and contest the rules on the basis of which their status is constituted. Owen argues that this links republican arguments against domination with cosmopolitan concerns that go beyond the protection of citizens of a state.

Lubomira Radoilska extends the discussion of domination to the conditions of integration for migrants who become citizens, more specifically the attitudes and dispositions that can be required of citizens. She argues that an integration policy that aims to integrate migrants into a national culture on the grounds that this is essential for interpersonal trust will lead to domination. This is so whether the model of trust is that of affective trust, requiring a primary attitude of trust to the other, or of cognitive trust, based on objective reasons for trusting the other. She argues in particular that the idea of a halfway position between those emphasizing only the rights of states or of migrants, a 'quasi contract' between existing citizens and immigrants, as advanced by David Miller, does not prevent domination, as it holds that the way immigrants can establish trustworthiness is to establish an identity that is separate from citizenship. Radoilska's argument suggests that a requirement for integration into the national culture is dominating on several grounds. First, the demand for integration in terms of 'identity' is indeterminate and essentially open-ended, as there is no clear fixed requirement for national identity. Second, cultural integration does not seem capable of overcoming the perception of migrants as politically untrustworthy where this exists. Finally, non-citizens, if not excluded, lack authority in the discourse about whether the current representation of national culture into which migrants should integrate is a reasonable norm. She concludes that the effect of grounding political trust in a shared national culture instead of democratic institutions would be to normalize the domination of immigrants and citizens alike.

Finally Christopher Bertram, addressing the broader issue of the balance of state sovereignty and individual freedom, brings together once more the two sets of migration issues – external and internal – arguing that controls on entry and on access to the rights and protections of citizenship can be seen as alternative strategies employed by contemporary states. He then examines the trade-off between migration controls and restrictions of access to resources within the country, comparing the harm of restricting freedom of movement into the country with that of excluding outsiders from social resources within the country. This draws on a social anthropological distinction between 'perimeter defence' and 'social boundary defence', identified as two alternative strategies for preserving their resources practised among forager groups. He argues that although much critique of contemporary immigration policy focuses on border controls, the restriction of resources to immigrants is equally widely practised both formally and informally. While, like Hovdal-Moan, acknowledging the value both of 'nationalist' goals of preserving collective autonomy and welfare and of cosmopolitan goals of protecting the basic rights and interests of all human beings, Bertram identifies problems of justice with both strategies. The perimeter defence strategy fails to treat all equally and may not be essential to support collective autonomy and welfare. The social boundary strategy violates the principles of democratic legitimacy and reciprocity and renders many vulnerable to exploitation. Thus, Bertram argues that we need to consider more closely the relative costs and benefits of these alternative strategies, and suggests that to citizens of modern states, territorial exclusion may seem superficially more acceptable than exclusion of those in the state from resources, but remains as problematic as the social boundary strategy.

Thus, these articles paint a complex picture with respect to the domination of migrants. The initial notion that migrants are vulnerable to domination gives way to a more differentiated and contested account of the kinds of domination to which migrants are subject. Vulnerability to domination varies among non-citizens, depending on their status and the costs of exit. While reducing domination of both would-be migrants and non-citizen residents of different statuses is seen as an important and feasible project, several articles suggest that full legal citizenship is not the only way in which protection from domination can be realized, or that it is rather elements of a disaggregated citizenship, along with a gradual pathway to full citizenship, that are required. At least two authors suggest that continuing domination of immigrants will have a dominating effect on citizens as well as non-citizens. Going further, the very power of states to construct and allocate non-citizen statuses, or to exclude entirely, may be seen as presenting higher level problems of domination. Yet, in promoting non-domination, there remain issues about what balance needs to be struck between providing for the collective autonomy of the 'free state' and protecting individuals and groups against domination that the state itself may exercise over non-citizen residents and would-be migrants.

Acknowledgements

The guest editors would like to acknowledge support from Phillip Cole and Gideon Calder for the workshops from which this special issue originated. They thank also all the speakers, respondents and participants at the Newport and Dublin workshops.

Funding

The guest editors are grateful for funding from the Social Ethics Research Group at the University of Wales, Newport, and from UCD's School of Politics and International Relations and College of Human Sciences; and to UCD Philosophy and Newman House for hosting the Dublin workshop.

Note

1. A claim to citizenship for resident non-citizens does not therefore follow directly from a procedural interpretation of arbitrariness, only that the laws and policies that apply to non-citizens are generally known, and 'enforced with absolute impartiality and procedural fairness' (Lovett 2012, p. 117).

Notes on contributors

Iseult Honohan is Senior Lecturer in the School of Politics and International Relations, University College Dublin. Her research interests lie in republican political theory and its applications, especially to the areas of diversity, migration and citizenship, on which she has published *Civic republicanism* (Routledge, 2002), two edited volumes, and a number of articles. She is a partner in EUDO Citizenship, the Citizenship strand of the European Union Observatory on Democracy.

Marit Hovdal-Moan is a postdoctoral research fellow at the Philosophy Department, Norwegian University of Science and Technology. Her research focuses primarily on normative approaches to international migration management, and the moral justifiability of state borders and boundaries. Her latest publication is 'Borders as a space of interaction: an account of special state obligations to irregular immigrants', *American behavioural scientist* (2012).

References

Abizadeh, A., 2008. Democratic theory and border coercion: no right to unilaterally control your own borders. *Political theory*, 36 (1), 37–65.

Bohman, J., 2007. *Democracy across borders: from demos to demoi*. Cambridge, MA: MIT Press.

Bohman, J., 2013. Kant, Madison and the problem of transnational order: popular sovereignty in multilevel systems. *In*: A. Niederberger and P. Schink, eds. *Republican democracy: liberty, law and politics*. Edinburgh: Edinburgh University Press, 62–88.

Carens, J., 1987. Aliens and citizens: the case for open borders. *Review of politics*, 49 (02), 251–273.

Carter, I., 1999. *A measure of freedom*. Oxford: Oxford University Press.

Carter, I., 2008. How are power and unfreedom related? *In*: C. Laborde and J. Maynor eds. *Republicanism and political theory*. Oxford: Blackwell.

Fine, S. Non-domination and the ethics of migration. *Critical review of international social and political philosophy*, 17 (1), 10–30.

Honohan, I., 2014. Domination and migration: an alternative approach to the legitimacy of migration controls. *Critical Review of International social and political philosophy*, 17 (1), 31–48.

Kramer, M., 2003. *The quality of freedom*. Oxford: Oxford University Press.

Kramer, M., 2008. Liberty and domination. *In*: C. Laborde and J. Maynor, eds. *Republicanism and political theory*. Oxford: Blackwell, 31–57.

Laborde, C., 2010. Republicanism and global justice: A sketch. *European journal of political theory*, 9 (1), 48–69.

Lovett, F., 2010. *A general theory of domination*. Oxford: Oxford University Press.

Markell, P., 2008. The insufficiency of non-domination. *Political theory*, 36 (1), 9–36.

McMahon, C., 2005. The indeterminacy of republican policy. *Philosophy and public affairs*, 33 (1), 67–93.

Pettit, P., 1997. *Republicanism*. Oxford: Oxford University Press.

Pettit, P., 2001. *A theory of freedom: from the psychology to the politics of agency*. New York: Oxford University Press.

Pettit, P., 2012. *On the people's terms: a republican theory and model of democracy*. Cambridge University Press.

Skinner, Q., 1998. *Liberty before liberalism*. Cambridge: Cambridge University Press.

Skinner, Q., 2008. Freedom as the absence of arbitrary power. *In*: C. Laborde and J. Maynor, eds. *Republicanism and political theory*. Oxford: Blackwell, pp., 83–101.

Non-domination and the ethics of migration

Sarah Fine

Philosophy, King's College London, London, UK

In this paper, I begin a preliminary exploration of the ways in which neo-Roman republicanism, organized as it is around the twin notions of free person and free state, might contribute to the ongoing conversation about the ethics of migration. I extrapolate and sketch distinctively republican responses to the following migration-related issues: refugees, resident non-citizens, international freedom of movement and state rights to exclude would-be immigrants. I indicate areas where I think republicans are on the strongest ground, areas where republicanism's contribution is limited and areas where republicans face important dilemmas. I examine how these dilemmas might be addressed from within republican theory. The aim is to reflect upon the ethics of migration through the lens of the neo-Roman conception of political liberty, to see what we learn both about enduring questions in the ethics of migration and about the appeal of contemporary republicanism as a political theory.

Introduction

The neo-Roman 'republican' tradition in political thought, recovered and revived by Quentin Skinner and Philip Pettit in particular, is now renowned for its distinctive conception of political liberty, and the intimate connection it draws between being a free person and living in a free state. In this paper, I begin a preliminary exploration of the ways in which neo-Roman-inspired republicanism, organized as it is around the twin notions of free person and free state, might contribute to the ongoing conversation about the ethics of migration.

I shall start with a basic introductory word or two about the neo-Roman republican tradition. The tradition has its roots in Roman political theory and law, (re)surfacing most notably in the political thought of Renaissance Italy, 17th- and 18th-century England, and 18th-century America. Its key figures include Niccolò Machiavelli, James Harrington, John Milton, Algernon Sydney, Richard Price, Montesquieu, Thomas Jefferson and James Madison

(Skinner 2002, Laborde and Maynor 2008a, Lovett and Pettit 2009). It is not to be confused with another strand of republican theory, which is more closely associated with Aristotelian political thought, and, latterly, with some contemporary communitarian thinkers, such as Michael Sandel (e.g. Sandel 1996).[1]

The figures within the neo-Roman tradition are united by a selection of shared views, foremost among them a distinctive understanding of political liberty. According to Skinner, the pre-eminent intellectual historian of neo-Roman republican political thought, the neo-Roman tradition is characterized by two slogans, which neatly summarize its two central commitments (Skinner 2010).[2] First, '*it is possible to act freely* [...] *if and only if you are a freeman*' (Skinner 2010, p. 98, author's emphasis). Second, '*it is possible to live and act as a freeman if and only if you live in a free state*' (Skinner 2010, p. 99, author's emphasis).

To elaborate, the focus for these republicans is on the related notions of free persons and free states (Pettit 2008, p. 103). A free person, a *liber homo*, is defined throughout this body of literature as 'the antonym of a slave' (Skinner 2008, p. 86). 'What it means to be a free person', Skinner explains, 'is *not to be dependent* – in the manner definitive of servitude – upon the will, and hence upon the mere goodwill, of anyone else' (Skinner 2010, p. 97, author's emphasis). People who are dependent in such a way are likely to self-censor, to make decisions on the basis of the master's preferences, and to be servile and accommodating (Skinner 2002, pp. 258–259). The neo-Roman conception of freedom is closely connected to the status of citizenship. Skinner continues:

> To be a freeman, the early-modern theorists affirm, is equivalent to being 'your own man', not beholden to a patron or a master, not the creature or dependant of anyone else. A freeman is consequently someone to be reckoned with, someone who can look you in the eye, who can reason and negotiate on terms of equality without ever feeling the need to doff the cap or bend the knee. As a result, freemen are said to enjoy the respect – and the self-respect – that comes of being known to speak frankly and behave without fear or favour, acting solely as reason and conscience dictate.
>
> (Skinner 2010, p. 97)

In addition, these thinkers are just as interested in the conditions necessary for securing and maintaining this kind of freedom, which in part explains the second slogan, that 'it is possible to live and act as a freeman if and only if you live in a free state' (p. 99). The free state, just like the free person, is independent, not subject to the will, the unchecked power, of any other agent. The free state acts in line with the will of its citizen body, not the will of a foreign power, and not just the will of a limited subset of its citizens. Thus, for example, a state is not free if it is controlled by a colonial regime, and it is not free if it is controlled by a despot who rules according to his own whim. Its subjects then would be at the mercy of an alien will, and thus enslaved: 'to live in such a predicament is what it means to live as a slave' (p. 100). Neo-Roman republicanism therefore offers a clear defence of self-government (of some description) and the rule of law.[3] Furthermore, free persons – citizens – must be willing to do what is required to uphold the freedom of the state, hence the neo-Roman republican emphasis on the instrumental importance of promoting civic virtue as a means to ensuring the health of the republic.[4]

The neo-Roman tradition is the inspiration behind contemporary neo-republicanism, which has been championed most famously, forcefully and systematically by Pettit, and which is oriented around this distinctive conception of liberty: a free person is 'one who does not live under the arbitrary will or domination of others' (Lovett and Pettit 2009, p. 12). A free state is 'one that promotes its citizens' freedom from domination, without itself coming to dominate them' (Lovett and Pettit 2009, p. 12). For contemporary neo-republicans (henceforth, republicans), freedom, in short, is the absence of domination or dependence. This republican understanding of freedom, then, is negative rather than positive, to use the familiar terminology; freedom is not equated with self-mastery. But republicans argue that their particular conception of freedom differs from the well-known negative view of freedom as the absence of interference, associated in its various forms with Thomas Hobbes, Jeremy Bentham, Isaiah Berlin and, in recent years, Matthew Kramer and Ian Carter.[5] For republicans, instead, X's freedom is not necessarily compromised by another's interference per se, but it is always compromised by the existence of some agent with the very power – not subject to X's control – to interfere arbitrarily in X's life. In Frank Lovett and Philip Pettit's words:

> I dominate you in a particular choice to the extent that I have the capacity, not subject to your direct or indirect check, to interfere in the choice, and I can employ that capacity to make it more probable, defiance apart, that you will choose to my pleasure or taste.
>
> (Lovett and Pettit 2009, p. 14)

Domination, therefore, may occur in the absence of any actual interference, as in the case of the slave with a non-interfering, benign master. Republicans point out that, whether or not the master leaves the slave with a range of options at his disposal, the slave is still a slave, the master still a master. There remains the ever-present possibility that the master might interfere, according to the master's whim, and it is this possibility, this power, that is pivotal in the slave's status as dominated, as unfree.

On the other hand, interference may occur in the absence of domination, and thus will not compromise freedom, as when citizens are bound by laws which are subject to the control (in some sense) of the citizens themselves, e.g. Harrington's famous 'empire of laws, and not of men'.[6] This obviously contrasts with Hobbes's notorious argument that the citizens of republican Luca are mistaken in their belief that their liberty is substantively different from or greater than that of the subjects of the sultan in Constantinople, 'for they fail to realise that what matters for individual liberty is not the source of the law but its extent' (Skinner 1997, p. 85). As Hobbes writes, 'whether a Common-wealth be Monarchical, or Popular, the Freedome is still the same' (Hobbes [1651] 1991, ch. 21; see also Laborde and Maynor 2008b, p. 4). Not so, according to republicans, for whom laws are not necessarily the enemies of individual freedom (Skinner 2010, p. 99). Worth noting here is a distinction that Pettit draws between factors that compromise freedom and factors that condition freedom (Pettit 2002, pp. 342–343). The undominating, non-arbitrary rule of law itself will not compromise freedom, but will condition it, in the sense of reducing 'the range or ease with which people enjoy undominated choice' (p. 342). In other words, the republican conception of freedom is not wholly indifferent to the presence of interference: the effective enjoyment of freedom will depend on 'the minimisation of intentional interference' (p. 343). But domination without interference is always qualitatively worse than interference without domination, because the former is freedom compromising, while the latter is not.

Contemporary republicans are committed to promoting 'the universal good of non-domination' at the individual and at the state level (Laborde 2010, p. 53). In that vein, they argue that states ought to pursue the kinds of policies that will further the goal of minimizing domination (e.g. Lovett and Pettit 2009, p. 20). On this point, Pettit also distinguishes between *imperium* (the public power of the state) and *dominium* (the private power of citizens). In order to minimize the domination of citizens by citizens, the state must restrain the effects of *dominium*, and this will require certain kinds of policies. But at the same time the citizens must also be protected from the state's *imperium* as a possible threat to freedom as non-domination, and this will require certain kinds of institutions (Pettit 2001, p. 153).[7]

In this paper, I will consider how contemporary republicans might approach some of the central questions in the ethics of migration. In particular, I will attempt to extrapolate and sketch distinctively republican responses to the following migration-related issues: refugees, resident non-citizens, international freedom of movement and state rights to exclude would-be immigrants. I will indicate areas where I think republicans are on the strongest ground and have the most to offer the debate, areas where republicanism seems to have little of distinction to add to the debate, or its contribution is ambiguous, and areas where republicans appear to face important dilemmas. I will also examine how these dilemmas might be addressed from within republican theory.

The argument presented here is not intended as a critical intervention in the ongoing philosophical debate about the concept of liberty, nor is it a contribution to internal republican disputes about how best to understand the concepts of domination or arbitrariness, for example, or about the exact relationship between contemporary republican theory and its neo-Roman antecedents. (There are, of course, internal differences in the contemporary republican camp, and I will comment upon those where they are relevant to the discussion at hand.)[8] Rather, the main aim is to reflect upon the ethics of migration through the lens of the neo-Roman conception of political liberty in order to see what we might learn both about enduring questions in the ethics of migration and about the appeal of contemporary republicanism as a political theory.

Statelessness, refugees and resident non-citizens

The ethics of international migration emerges as a subject of profound political, and profoundly political, importance precisely within the context of an international state system, characterized by the existence of separate sovereign states, which claim the authority to control various aspects of the movement of people into and out of the territory under their jurisdiction. If there were no such international state system, or if states did not claim authority to control the movement of people across state borders, then we would be talking about something else instead. Republican political theory, with its emphasis on political liberty – on what it is to be a free person in connection with membership of a free state – and its acknowledgement of the enduring (and enduringly pivotal) role of states, seems in some respects particularly well placed to approach a variety of questions in the ethics of migration.

Unsurprisingly, republicanism appears well equipped to diagnose at least some of the distinctive ills that can accompany the precarious status of certain classes of migrant in certain contexts. Over half a century ago, Hannah Arendt – a republican, though not one of the neo-Roman variety – penned what remains the seminal work on the condition of statelessness and refugees, the most pressing (because most desperate) issue in the ethics of migration (Arendt 1951, ch. 9). 'Man, it turns out', she wrote, 'can lose all so-called Rights of Man without losing his essential quality as man, his human dignity. Only the loss of a polity itself expels him from humanity' (p. 297). Arendt's historically sensitive argument is rich and complex, but one of the essential messages is that in a world wholly divided up into nation-states, to speak of a person's so-called natural or human rights is entirely meaningless in the absence of a state willing (or another agent able) to protect and enforce them; lacking state membership – citizenship, nationality – means lacking the very 'right to have rights'. The fact that states claim complete control over issues of membership conspires to leave us with a class of people who are denied membership anywhere, and, correspondingly, effectively have no rights at all. Interestingly, Arendt employs language that calls to mind the neo-Roman conception of liberty, when she writes, regarding 20th-century European totalitarian regimes, of 'the powerful position which the police had achieved over the years in their unrestricted and arbitrary domination of stateless and refugees' (p. 289). The condition of statelessness, a person with no state membership and no state protection in a world of states, is the most precarious, powerless position possible. It is worse than slavery (p. 297). It seems to represent the very epitome of insecurity and subjection to domination:

domination by the expelling or denationalizing state, domination by officials within or at the borders of other states, domination by private citizens – employers, landlords, traffickers, and so on. The stateless person is certainly not expected to 'behave without fear or favour' (Skinner 2010, p. 97). Indeed, vulnerability to domination seems to capture one of the key evils of the condition of statelessness, and, moreover, the stateless person in a world of states appears to confirm the truth in Skinner's two republican slogans, that 'it is possible to act freely [...] if and only if you are a freeman', and that 'it is possible to live and act as a freeman if and only if you live in a free state' (pp. 98–99). It highlights an element of what is always insufficient about the temporary solution of refugee camps: even if the most basic subsistence needs are or can be met (which evidently is not the case in many refugee camps), the problem of domination still persists so long as people do not have access to membership and the proper protection of a state, as well as protection against the possible excesses of state power. If the status of the free and equal citizen in a free state is the guiding vision of republican political theory, then the condition of statelessness in a world of states is something of a republican nightmare.

Since republicans are concerned with minimizing the risk of domination, then the enduring problem of statelessness and refugees must be a top priority. Arendt was the first to point out that no straightforward political solution is forthcoming in practice. In principle, however, the neo-Roman republican answer presumably is that the promotion of non-domination requires that everyone ought to have access to citizenship in a state, and ultimately a free state, somewhere.[9] Since the core problem of statelessness is the problem of lacking citizenship – state membership – in a world made up of states, it is a problem with a clear *theoretical* solution, one that fits nicely within the republican formula of free person in free state. It is not unexpected, of course, that a political theory so closely associated with (the value of) citizenship in a self-governing state can clearly diagnose some of the dangers and power deficits that accompany the status of lacking citizenship anywhere.

Republicanism is similarly comfortable, even forceful, on the subject and the status of resident non-citizens, or 'denizens'. In her innovative work on denizenship, Meghan Benton draws on and develops the republican conception of freedom as non-domination to deliver a compelling account of the precise ways in which denizens in general, and different subgroups of denizens in particular, are vulnerable to domination (Benton 2010a, 2010b, 2014). She highlights the degree to which denizens (both in comparison and in contrast with citizens) are subject to the power of the state in which they are resident, including, importantly, the fact that the state 'holds transformative power over the status of migrants', in the sense that it can detain and deport them, for example. This, she argues, ought to be of paramount concern for republicans, who wish to minimize domination. Indeed, Benton is right to wonder why contemporary republicans have not paid more attention to the subject of denizens.[10] She constructs an argument about the exact conditions in which denizenship is problematic, because potentially dominating, focusing on the costs of leaving the status of denizenship (either by leaving the state or by becoming a citizen). Again, Benton's republican emphasis on the ills accompanying domination appears as an especially effective backdrop for the examination of the status of some migrants, capturing much of what makes certain subgroups – undocumented migrants, migrants from poor and weak states, unskilled migrants, for instance – especially vulnerable, and their position especially concerning.

In a sense, the republican account is able to offer a sophisticated, nuanced, more differentiated analysis or reconstruction of Michael Walzer's emotive response to the challenging case of guest workers. Walzer writes, in tones at times reminiscent of contemporary republicanism:

> These guests experience the state as a pervasive and frightening power that shapes their lives and regulates their every move – and never asks their opinion. Departure is only a formal option; deportation, a continuous practical threat. As a group, they constitute a disenfranchised class. They are typically an exploited or oppressed class as well, and they are exploited or oppressed at least in part because they are disenfranchised, incapable of organizing effectively for self-defense. [...] The relevant principle here is not mutual aid but political justice. The guests don't need citizenship – at least not in the same sense in which they might be said to need their jobs. Nor are they injured, helpless, destitute; they are able-bodied and earning money. Nor are they standing, even figuratively, by the side of the road; they are living among the citizens. They do socially necessary work, and they are deeply enmeshed in the legal system of the country to which they have come. Participants in economy and law, they ought to be able to regard themselves as potential or future participants in politics as well. [...] They must be set on the road to citizenship. They may choose not to become citizens, to return home or to stay on as resident aliens. [...] But unless they have that choice, their other choices cannot be taken as so many signs of their acquiescence to the economy and law of the countries where they work.
>
> (Walzer 1983, pp. 59–60)

In fact, another element of Walzer's argument with republican undertones is his claim that the co-existence of members and permanent non-members within a state is unavoidably corrosive of that state's democratic ideals, including its supposed commitment to freedom and equality. As he puts it, 'the determination of aliens and guests by an exclusive band of citizens (or of slaves by masters, or women by men, or blacks by whites, or conquered peoples by their conquerors) is not communal freedom but oppression' (p. 62). Ultimately, it is bad for citizens and non-citizens alike. This is reminiscent of a recurrent republican theme, which emerged in response to colonialism and imperialism, that there is a kind of negative feedback loop: states that dominate abroad will become corrupt at home too.[11] In short, a state that engages in practices of domination not only threatens the free status of the dominated parties, but also threatens its very standing as a free state. The free status of state residents, then, is intimately tied to the free status of the state – a connection that runs in both directions.[12]

So potential republican responses to topics in the ethics of migration are at their strongest and most compelling when the threat or presence of domination is clear and pressing; when the issue of status is central, for example, when the type of migrant status itself signals or represents a clear imbalance of power, affecting the migrant's ability to live as a free person, enjoying the ability and security to plan for the future, to behave without 'fear or favour'; and when there is a theoretical solution that somehow clearly connects the status of free person and the status of free state (as in the demand for access to citizenship in a state). These are among the least morally controversial areas in the ethics of migration – even philosophical defenders of the state's right to exclude would-be immigrants can agree that refugees and undocumented migrants, for example, are particularly vulnerable to domination, though they inevitably will disagree about how best to address that domination and what this situation requires of states.

The broad appeal of a republican response to the urgent problems of statelessness, refugees and the position of some resident non-citizens calls to mind Cécile Laborde's contention that her brand of critical republicanism in particular, with its emphasis on the importance of 'resistance to concrete forms of unjust power', in some ways resembles a Judith Skhlar style 'liberalism of fear', primarily aimed at 'combat[ing] the bad rather than promot[ing] the good' (Laborde 2010, p. 50). The republican conception of freedom as non-domination, then, is especially relevant when there is something clearly problematic to be addressed, something 'bad' to be combated, some form of unjust power to be resisted.

International freedom of movement

On the other hand, republicanism's strength in the face of urgent, power-deficit problems does not necessarily translate into quite so obvious a strength with respect to less seemingly urgent, dramatic or *obviously* morally troubling migration-related issues – the kinds of issues that rarely figure in popular discussions about migration, the kinds of migration policies whose justification people tend to take for granted now. (This is not so much a criticism as an observation; indeed, perhaps it speaks in favour of republicanism that it is on firmest territory when confronted with the most urgent moral and political questions.) One of the central and more contentious debates in the academic literature – if not in popular discussions – on the ethics of migration revolves around the question of whether there is or ought to be a human right to international freedom of movement (see, for example, the disagreement between Oberman forthcoming, and Miller forthcoming. See also Cole 2000, and Oberman 2009).[13] If one takes the rival negative view that freedom consists in the absence of interference, and coercively enforced immigration restrictions evidently represent an obstruction, a hindrance, a form of interference in the choices of would-be immigrants, an avoidable narrowing of their potential options, then immigration restrictions are to that extent freedom compromising with regard to would-be immigrants. For libertarians and for some liberals, any freedom restricting move triggers a demand for justification of some sort – the onus is on those who wish to interfere with individual choices (and, in this case, sovereign states are the interfering parties) to show why that interference is justifiable. The default position would be international freedom of movement – more rather than less freedom – unless some justification can be found for state imposed restrictions on movement. Then the disagreement is over whether or not a suitable justification for freedom limiting restrictive immigration policies is forthcoming, what sort of justification counts as suitable, and so forth. That is not to say, of course, that all those who hold the view that freedom consists in the absence of interference also must believe that there is or ought to be a human right to international freedom of movement all things considered, but just that they must recognize barriers to international freedom of movement as freedom compromising.[14]

From the standpoint of a republican conception of freedom as the absence of domination, however, matters are not quite so clear-cut. It is not immediately obvious that immigration restrictions are always freedom compromising, even if they are freedom conditioning, in Pettit's terminology. Republicans do not start from the assumption that any specific instance of interference in individual choices is freedom compromising and in need of justification. While immigration restrictions do count as interference, and inevitably limit the potential options from which would-be immigrants (indeed, any non-citizens) may choose, they are only freedom compromising on a republican understanding of freedom if domination is also present.[15] The default position, absent further justification, therefore, is not necessarily international freedom of movement. We would need to know whether – and, if so, where – domination enters the picture.[16]

To develop that line of enquiry, the paper now turns to a foundational question in the ethics of migration, namely, whether states enjoy a general moral right to exclude would-be immigrants from their territory and from acquiring citizenship.[17] This issue appears to pose an interesting challenge for republican theory, for two main reasons. First, the republican's traditional focus is on the free person in a free state. Is the freedom of the individual compromised by *imperium* and/or *dominium*? Is the freedom of the state compromised by internal or external forces, which in turn compromise the freedom of the citizens? The republican's traditional remedies always have been some combination of self-government, the rule of law, policies to minimize domination between citizens, the instrumental importance of civic virtue in sustaining the republic, and so forth. Here, however, the question is whether the freedom of the would-be immigrant is compromised by states other than her own (not qua citizen, and not by fellow citizens). The would-be immigrants' state of citizenship may be entirely unaffected by the supposed domination of its citizens by foreign states. Does this different set-up call for a different set of answers, or do traditional republican answers apply in this context, too?

Second, the republican's slogans emphasize the fundamental importance of the free state: it is possible to be a free person only if one lives in a free state. Yet, in the case of the state's supposed right to exclude, there seems to be potential for domination on both sides of the equation – the domination of would-be immigrants, where states enjoy complete authority over immigration decisions, or the domination of states, where these states do *not* enjoy complete authority over immigration decisions. If that is right, then it is not clear which way the republican should turn in the quest to minimize domination.

The right to exclude

First, how might the republican approach the particular issue of state immigration control, given that it seems to raise questions outside and beyond the familiar republican territory of the free citizen of the free state? As a point of departure, we can examine how republicans address other pressing matters beyond state borders. A number of contemporary republican political theorists are in the process of developing republican responses to international issues, including, for example, questions of global justice, global governance, human rights and the challenges presented by current manifestations of globalization (e.g. Bohman 2008, Ivison 2010, Laborde 2010, Laborde and Ronzoni forthcoming). As Laborde points out, these attempts might be met with some initial scepticism, particularly since republicanism is usually considered to understand 'freedom as citizenship in a bounded community' (Laborde 2010, p. 49). However, Laborde maintains that republicanism actually offers 'a useful paradigm for normative reflection on what James Bohman has called the new global circumstances of politics' (p. 50). As she explains:

> [...] The current international order is marked by one-sided and largely coerced domination and dependency. Just as republicans have historically pointed to the evils of arbitrary power in sub-state units such as the workplace and the family, they, similarly, can point to the evil of transnational domination, be it by states, corporations, or international organizations. (p. 50)

Laborde argues further that we ought to focus not only on the domination that occurs within 'interpersonal relationships', but also on the domination within 'basic, systemic power structures' (p. 54). In the global picture, we should pay close attention to the fact that the international system represents 'a (structurally unfair) systemic order which authorizes and aggravates the pre-institutional subservience and dependency of weak states' (p. 57).

One option, then, is to show how republican political theory, with its distinctive conception of freedom as the absence of domination, is just as insightful and illuminating on global political questions – its relevance extends well beyond borders. Laborde's account, for example, focuses on how weak, poor states are dominated in the context of the current global system, and, thus, by extension, how their citizens suffer from the power imbalance, as well as the ways in which wealthier states and their citizens benefit from the structurally unfair order and the unjust international institutions that they share responsibility for upholding (e.g. pp. 58–59). Free person and free state are still interconnected and harmonious, rather than potentially in conflict. The solution is to reduce the domination suffered by weak, poor states, which in turn will reduce the domination of their citizens. What is more, Skinner portrays Laborde's argument as a good example of how the second neo-Roman slogan – 'it is possible to live and act as a freeman if and only if you live in a free state' – can be used effectively to extend the reach of republican theory into discussions of international justice (Skinner 2010, p. 101). As Skinner outlines one step in Laborde's argument:

> [...] When a state is dominated, one consequence is that it loses its freedom to act according to its own will in the organization of its affairs. But this is to say that its citizens are reduced to living in dependence on the goodwill of persons who are outside their control, but who nevertheless exercise alien control over each and every one of them. To live in a dominated state is thus to forfeit one's own individual liberty at the same time. (p. 101)

It employs familiar republican resources to address contemporary concerns. A similar 'updating' argument is outlined by Pettit:

> According to standard republican doctrine, individuals are meant to enjoy freedom as non-domination in virtue of being protected against the domination of others by an undominating state. What we now see is that this actually leaves something out. For those individuals will not be fully free if their state is dominated by other states. A full statement of the requirements for individual freedom, under a constitutional arrangement, should read: the free individual is protected against the domination of others by the undominating and undominated state. It is the requirement that the state be undominated that explains why the domination of suitable states is *pro tanto* bad.
>
> (Pettit 2010, p. 77)[18]

More recently, Laborde and Miriam Ronzoni have developed a detailed account of the ways in which the 'circumstances of global politics' open up a range of avenues for the domination of states (not just weak and poor ones) by other states and non-state actors. They argue that republican political theory offers 'a plausible and attractive ideal for global justice: the internationalist ideal of the free state'. They point precisely to Skinner's two slogans, and the significance of the free state (Laborde and Ronzoni forthcoming).

How, then, might these internationalist republicans deal with the distinctive case of the would-be immigrant versus a prospective receiving state? Following Iseult Honohan, the republican might wish to draw on the internationalist republican arguments to illustrate the precise ways in which would-be immigrants may be dominated by unilaterally imposed and unchecked immigration controls. Honohan adopts Frank Lovett's definition of domination, according to which 'persons or groups are subject to domination to the extent that they are dependent on a social relationship in which some other person or group wields arbitrary power over them' (Honohan 2014, p. 34, citing Lovett 2010, p. 119). With that definition of domination, as Honohan notes, would-be immigrants are subject to domination to the extent that 'they are in a relationship of dependence with the countries which exclude them'. In the contemporary world, she argues, we can see a relationship of dependence 'in the context of those asymmetrical power relationships in which people are dependent on and subject to the arbitrary power of corporations, wealthier states, international organisations and others' (Honohan 2014, p. 41). Against that background relationship, we may view the state's unilateral right to exclude would-be immigrants, according to its own discretion, as a potential, significant source or link in a chain of domination (varying in intensity and extent in different cases and contexts, depending on the kinds of exclusionary measures in use, and the circumstances of the migrants in question). Accordingly, given their goal of minimizing domination, the republican's preliminary prescription would be:

> establishing the legal status of migrants, and recognising their equality in respects other than admission; applying the rule of law to migration controls by limiting arbitrary powers and constraining discretionary procedures; making accountable the institutions determining migration law and policies by the introduction of a higher regulatory authority; and finally making migration law and policy contestable in some way by those who are subjected to them.
>
> (Honohan 2014, p. 42)

The argument that would-be immigrants are dominated in some sense in relation to (unilaterally imposed) immigration controls seems a powerful one. Recall the Lovett and Pettit basic definition of domination:

> I dominate you in a particular choice to the extent that I have the capacity, not subject to your direct or indirect check, to interfere in the choice, and I can employ that capacity to make it more probable, defiance apart, that you will choose to my pleasure or taste.
>
> (Lovett and Pettit 2009, p. 14)

This definition seems to describe quite perfectly the relationship between prospective receiving state and would-be immigrant. The receiving state has the capacity, not subject (or at least not usually subject) to the immigrant's direct or indirect check, to interfere in the would-be immigrant's choice to migrate, and the state can employ that capacity to make it more probable, defiance apart, that the would-be immigrant will choose to the state's pleasure or taste. In other words, the relationship between receiving state and would-be immigrant seems to constitute a crystal clear case of domination. The would-be immigrant is subject to the power of the prospective receiving state, a power that the immigrant experiences as arbitrary. It is true, of course, that would-be immigrants may not be completely powerless or voiceless vis-à-vis the receiving state. Their interests may be championed by already resident family and community members, immigrant advocacy and pressure groups or sympathetic politicians within the state, or by politicians and officials from their own state, or regional and international organizations, for example. Nonetheless, the potential for domination seems undeniable, since immigration policy is not subject to the control or contestation of would-be immigrants themselves, but appears to signal the capacity of the state to interfere arbitrarily in the would-be immigrants' choices.

Before concluding that the republican case in favour of regulating state control over immigration is unambiguous, though, consider another of Walzer's well-known arguments about migration and membership:

> The distribution of membership is not pervasively subject to the constraints of justice. Across a considerable range of the decisions that are made, states are simply free to take in strangers (or not) – as much as they are free, leaving aside the claims of the needy, to share their wealth with foreign friends, to honor the achievements of foreign artists, scholars, and scientists, to choose their trading partners, and to enter into collective security arrangements with other states. But the right to choose an admissions policy is more basic than any of these, for it is not merely a matter of acting in the world, exercising sovereignty, and pursuing national interests. At stake here is the shape of the community that acts in the world, exercises sovereignty, and so on. Admission and exclusion are at the core of communal independence. They suggest the deepest meaning of self-determination.
>
> (Walzer 1983, pp. 61–62)

This has proven to be one of the most controversial aspects of Walzer's work on the subject, setting up and spelling out his support for a (limited) right to exclude would-be immigrants. However, the idea of admission and exclusion as central to communal independence also appears to tie in with certain republican themes and commitments. Recall that the republican free state is cast as independent, not subject to the will, the unchecked control, of any other agent. The free state acts in accordance with the will of its citizens, *all* of them and *only* them, thus protecting and enabling the citizens' freedom. It seems that control over admissions policy is something that a genuinely free state, in the republican mould, would wish to claim for itself and its citizens. Who or what else is entitled to make these decisions on behalf of the state and its citizens?

Indeed, in one respect, the idea of admission and exclusion as pivotal to communal independence seems to have important anti-colonialist implications. The archetypal republican free state is one that is independent of alien control, especially in the form of colonial rule, and to ensure itself against colonialist advances and the subsequent 'enslavement' of its population, the free state must be able to exclude potential colonisers. Furthermore, republicans famously are concerned with protecting citizens from the state's *imperium* as a possible threat to freedom as non-domination. Presumably, however, institutions designed to regulate the behaviour of states also have the potential to abuse their powers and to constitute a threat to freedom of states and their citizens alike. It follows that republicans should be just as, if not more, wary of the powers of international and supra-national institutions.

On the one hand, then, the state's right to exclude seems to leave would-be immigrants subject to domination; on the other hand, the state's right to exclude would-be immigrants appears to have a clear, even compelling, *republican* justification, in line with the requirements and entitlements of free, independent states.

An initial thought might be that any apparent dilemma for the republican simply dissolves on closer inspection, because there is only domination or the risk thereof on one or other side of the divide, or because the risk of domination is obviously far greater on one side of the divide – in which case it would be clear which direction the republican should turn in the quest to minimize domination.

For instance, one might question the extent to which would-be immigrants stand in a relationship of dependence with prospective receiving states such that they are properly construed as dominated by the power of the state to exclude them. Or one might agree that at least some would-be immigrants are dominated by the power of the state to exclude them, but still maintain that the overall goal of minimizing domination is not necessarily best served by limiting state discretion over immigration control and, for example, granting a 'higher regulatory authority' the power to oversee immigration law (Honohan 2014, p. 42). It might be, as Pettit has argued, that 'there are all sorts of ways in which it may be quite natural to tolerate a political failure to honour non-domination, if the failure represents the most effective means to honour non-domination overall' (Pettit 1997, p. 102). It is worth emphasizing that this kind of argument is, of course, compatible with the claim that the state's supposed right to exclude lacks justification or remains problematic for other reasons; it might just be that the problem here is not best or most usefully characterized in terms of domination per se, and/or that the broader pursuit of non-domination is not best served by interventions which include, for example, devolving a subset of existing state powers to external institutions.

Conversely, regarding the other side of the dilemma, one might maintain, with Honohan, that restricting the state's control over immigration does not actually threaten its standing as a free state in the relevant sense. Or, again, the republican might recognize the potential for domination on both sides, but argue that, while regulating state control of immigration would compromise the freedom of the state, in fact it *would* be the best method for furthering the wider goal of non-domination.

Nonetheless, an important republican warning of sorts is sounded by Laborde and Ronzoni, in their discussion of why the state has been and remains so important for republicans. Republicans, they argue, in line with Pettit:

> have reason to value the particular quality of non-domination that can exclusively be achieved within democratically organized polities. Democracies are (archetypically) free states. Domestically, the best way for power not to be arbitrary is for it to embody, or at least be controlled by, the will of the people themselves.
>
> (Laborde and Ronzoni forthcoming, p. 21)

In short, the republican who calls for a rethinking of state control over immigration must also think very carefully about the ways in which the proposals can accommodate other essential aspects of the republican vision, most notably a state controlled by the will of the people themselves, and a community of equal citizens.[19]

A cosmopolitan turn

As an alternative move, the republican considering the ethics of migration might consider taking a more cosmopolitan turn, moving beyond the free person-free state mantra, in the manner of James Bohman. For Bohman, given the multiple forms of domination perpetuated by and within the current international system, the republican commitment to reducing domination – the pursuit of 'robust nondomination' – requires the establishment of a federal 'republic of humanity', a 'republic of republics', dispersing and diffusing power vertically and horizontally across a range of institutions (Bohman 2008, pp. 190–191, 200). Otherwise, the concern is that 'the power exercised in any particular institution is ultimately democratically arbitrary', because unchecked by those outside the decision-making body but still subject to its power, and so 'citizens become dominators of other citizens' (p. 201). Hence, the conditions necessary for securing and maintaining freedom as non-domination go well beyond securing non-domination within state borders.

Bohman maintains that the republicanism of the 17th- and 18th-century 'Commonwealthman', so central to Skinner's and Pettit's arguments, contained profoundly elitist elements, and that contemporary republicans should look instead to the transnationalism of later Enlightenment, anti-colonial republican thinkers, and to a suitably revised conception of domination. Instead of focusing on the idea of a free person in a free state, then, Bohman is able to broaden the republican argument substantially by rewording the classic statement: 'to be free is to be the citizen of a free *community*' (p. 203, emphasis added). The free community he has in mind is not confined to the traditional nation-state but rather is the community of humanity as a whole. As he contends, 'robust nondomination now requires membership in many different interacting and interrelated political communities, which together constitute the republic of humanity' (p. 215).

Bohman's transnational republicanism appears to offer a means of dissolving any apparent republican dilemma regarding state immigration controls, which might seem to count in its favour. His position recognizes the potential for bounded democratic republics to dominate would-be immigrants, for example, through arbitrary, unchecked control. Yet states need not claim a unilateral right to exclude would-be immigrants in order to avoid ceding control to outside forces and thus subjecting themselves to external domination. What is required, instead, are the kinds of international institutions, arrangements and relationships that provide for democratic rights (and acknowledge obligations) beyond the state. Rules will not be imposed either on states or on individuals (such as would-be immigrants) without their having an opportunity to participate in the making of those rules at some level. The rules will not be arbitrary. In effect, republicans are not forced to choose between the non-domination of the receiving state and the non-domination of the would-be immigrant. With the appropriate international arrangements, the non-domination of all can be secured.

This possible method of dissolving the dilemma is not without its costs and complications for republicans, though. For a start, this form of republican cosmopolitanism obviously deviates from the traditional republican emphasis on the freedom of the state. But on the traditional model, the citizenry are there to guard against the excesses of public power, and public power guards against the misuse of private power. Does the republican cosmopolitan model offer an appealing and plausible redrawing of that picture? It must grapple with all the usual and not inconsiderable practical cosmopolitan challenges (indeed, the same is true for internationalist republicans) – most notably, how to ensure that international and transnational institutions are sufficiently accountable to those subject to their control. It is no good having a federal republic of humanity, with power dispersed across and within a range of international institutions, if the powers are not subject to proper democratic checks and if ordinary citizens do not have some degree of control over the actions of those institutions. Bohman often draws on the European Union as a model for transnational democratic governance, but the problem of democratic accountability with respect to European institutions certainly has not yet been addressed to the satisfaction of many European citizens (e.g. Bohman 2008, p. 200).

Then there is the added, distinctively republican challenge, too, which is how to promote the kind of civic virtue necessary to ensure that citizens are willing to protect and maintain the relevant republican institutions, and sustain the republic in good health. As Laborde points out, 'the traditional argument would conclude [that] republican cosmopolitanism is an oxymoron because, at the global level, it is not possible to reproduce the practices, institutions and virtue essential to founding and maintaining republics' (Laborde 2010, p. 49). This challenge may not be insurmountable (we already know that federal republics can be substantial in size, as in the example of the United States), but it is a significant challenge all the same, and one which is particularly acute for a political theory born in the very different context of ancient city states.[20]

Conclusion

The ethics of international migration raises a host of difficult and important questions for political theorists. In this paper, I have begun to explore how neo-Roman republicans might approach some of those questions. When characterized as a theory oriented around a conception of freedom as non-domination, and committed to the twin principles that 'it is possible to act freely [...] if and only if you are a freeman' and that 'it is possible to live and act as a freeman if and only if you live in a free state', republicanism seems particularly well placed to address pressing migration issues regarding statelessness, refugees, and resident non-citizens. At the same time, though, and for the same reasons, it appears to have more difficulty with the issue of the freedom of would-be immigrants versus the freedom of prospective receiving states. It may even face something of a dilemma, one which might be dissolved but at the expense of reconfiguring the core relationship between the free person and the free state.

There is, as ever, more to be said on each of the issues raised in this paper. In addition, initial impressions suggest that republican theory might offer interesting and distinctive contributions to other subjects in the ethics of migration that I have not discussed here – the freedom to emigrate, and the rights of non-resident citizens, for example.[21] There is a lot more to think about. I hope to have shown that examining the ethics of migration through the lens of republicanism promises to bring into a view a range of new insights, both for migration research and for republicanism itself as a contemporary political theory engaged with contemporary political problems.

Acknowledgements

I would like to thank the participants at the workshop on 'Domination, Migration, and Non-Citizens', held at University College Dublin, 20 April 2012, for a very helpful discussion of the paper. Particular thanks to my discussant Marit Hovdal-Moan. Thanks also to Duncan Bell, Robert Jubb, Iseult Honohan and to the journal referees. The invitation from Iseult and Marit to participate in the workshop prompted me to think about this question from the perspective of an interested observer. The first draft of the paper was written while I was a Research Fellow at Corpus Christi College, Cambridge.

Notes

1. For discussion of various other important aspects of republican political thought, see also van Gelderen and Skinner (2002), Nabulsi (1999), esp. ch. 6, and Bell (2009).

2. Skinner himself prefers not to use the term 'republican' to describe the neo-Roman tradition of thought. However, following Philip Pettit, 'republican' is now widely used in that way, and Skinner acknowledges that he 'seems to have lost this part of the argument' (Skinner 2008, p. 84).
3. Self-government 'of some description' because, as Skinner highlights, a number of the early modern writers within this tradition were advocates of mixed government, with elements of monarchical, aristocratic and democratic control, and were perfectly comfortable with the idea of a self-governing community under the rule of monarch – hence, Skinner's resistance to describing this as a specifically *republican* tradition (Skinner 1997, pp. 53–55).
4. For further elaboration, see Skinner (1997) and Lovett and Pettit (2009), esp. p. 23.
5. On the distinctiveness of the neo-Roman conception, see especially Skinner (1997). On the non-interference negative conception, see, for example, Carter (1999) and Kramer (2003).
6. The phrase is repeated throughout the republican literature (e.g. Pettit 2002, p. 345; and Lovett and Pettit 2009, p. 12).
7. For critical discussion, see McMahon (2005).
8. On internal differences, see, for example, Bohman (2008), in which Bohman highlights some of his differences with Pettit and Skinner. On this issue, see also Benton (2010b).
9. But, as Marit Hovdal-Moan pointed out in her comments to me, which states? Who has responsibility for whom? Which agents may or should act to ensure that stateless people can acquire citizenship somewhere? These are just some of the questions that republicans must confront on the subject of refugees and statelessness.
10. Exceptions include Bohman (2007). Although note Robert Goodin's argument about the exclusionary history of republics. Here he quotes John Dryzek: 'Republics [...] could flourish as a result of their exclusion and exploitation of slaves, noncitizens and women. Republican citizenship and public freedom for the few was bought at the expense of excluding the many' (Goodin 2003, p. 62).
11. On this point, see Bohman (2008). See also Bell (2009).
12. Though again see Goodin's argument about the exclusionary, elitist history of republics, in Goodin (2003).
13. The seminal defence of international freedom of movement is Carens (1987).
14. For further discussion on the subject of freedom as the absence of interference and the right to freedom of movement, see Stilz (forthcoming).
15. In other words, it is not clear to me that, according to the republican, 'migration controls are prima facie dominating' (see Honohan in this issue).
16. Note here Arash Abizadeh's now well-known argument that unilaterally imposed immigration restrictions subject would-be immigrants to coercion and invade their 'autonomy', triggering a demand for democratic justification. The conditions of autonomy are understood in Razian terms, as follows: 'the person (1) has the appropriate mental capacities to formulate personal projects and pursue them, (2) enjoys an adequate range of valuable options, and (3) is independent, that is, free from subjection to the will of another through coercion or manipulation'. The third condition has parallels with the republican conception of freedom as non-domination, but the inclusion of the second condition – the adequate range of valuable options – indicates that autonomy can be compromised just by means of reducing the range of options open to a person, such that the range is no longer 'adequate'. This appears to give Abizadeh stronger grounds than the 'non-domination'

republican for claiming that unilateral immigration restrictions are freedom compromising and stand in need of justification (Abizadeh 2008, pp. 39–40).
17. For an in-depth discussion of this question, see Fine (forthcoming). See also Fine (2010).
18. Note Skinner's response to this: 'I cannot agree that the early-modern theorists leave out the consideration that Pettit rightly highlights. […] But Pettit is undoubtedly right that we cannot, according to the theorists I have been discussing, consider ourselves in possession of our liberty unless we live as citizens of a state which is free not merely from internal domination by monarchs or oligarchies, but also from external domination by other states' (Skinner 2010, p. 100).
19. For an attempt to grapple with these kinds of questions, from a democratic perspective, see Fine (forthcoming), ch. 2.
20. For more on this point, see Fine (2011).
21. On the issue of emigration, see the very interesting discussions in Stilz (forthcoming) and Wellman (forthcoming). On non-resident citizens, see Bauböck (2009) and Owen (2009).

Notes on contributor

Sarah Fine is a Lecturer in Philosophy at King's College London. She has written widely on migration and citizenship. Her monograph, *Immigration and the right to exclude*, is forthcoming with Oxford University Press. She is co-editor of a volume (with Lea Ypi), *Migration in political theory: the ethics of movement and membership*, also forthcoming with Oxford University Press.

References

Abizadeh, A., 2008. Democratic theory and border coercion: no right to unilaterally control your own borders. *Political theory*, 36 (1), 37–65.

Arendt, H., 1951. *The origins of totalitarianism*. New York: Harcourt.

Bauböck, R., 2009. The rights and duties of external citizenship. *Citizenship studies*, 13 (5), 475–499.

Bell, D., 2009. Republican imperialism: J.A. Froude and the virtue of empire. *History of political thought*, 30 (1), 166–191.

Benton, M., 2010a. The tyranny of the enfranchised majority? the accountability of states to their non-citizen population. *Res publica*, 16 (4), 397–413.

Benton, M., 2010b. A theory of denizenship. Thesis (PhD). University College London.

Benton, M., 2014. The problem of denizenship: a non-domination framework. *Critical review of international social and political philosophy*, 17 (1), 49–69.

Bohman, J., 2007. *Democracy across borders: from dêmos to dêmoi*. Cambridge MA: MIT Press.

Bohman, J., 2008. Nondomination and transnational democracy. *In*: C. Laborde and J. Maynor, eds. *Republicanism and political theory*. Oxford: Blackwell, 190–216.

Carens, J.H., 1987. Aliens and citizens: the case for open borders. *The review of politics*, 49 (2), 251–273.

Carter, I., 1999. *A measure of freedom*. Oxford: Oxford University Press.

Cole, P., 2000. *Philosophies of exclusion: liberty political theory and immigration*. Edinburgh: Edinburgh University Press.

Fine, S., 2010. Freedom of association is not the answer. *Ethics*, 120 (2), 338–356.

Fine, S., 2011. Democracy, citizenship and the bits in between. *Critical review of international social and political philosophy*, 14 (5), 623–640.

Fine, S., forthcoming. *Immigration and the right to exclude.* Oxford: Oxford University Press.

van Gelderen, M. and Skinner, Q., eds., 2002. *Republicanism: a shared European heritage. Volumes I and II.* Cambridge: Cambridge University Press.

Goodin, R.E., 2003. Folie républicaine. *Annual review of political science*, 6 (1), 55–76.

Hobbes, T., [1651] 1991. *Leviathan.* ed. R. Tuck. Cambridge: Cambridge University Press.

Honohan, I., 2014. Domination and migration: an alternative approach to the legitimacy of migration controls. *Critical review of international social and political philosophy*, 17 (1), 31–48.

Ivison, D., 2010. Republican human rights? *European Journal of Political Theory*, 9 (1), 31–47.

Kramer, M., 2003. *The quality of freedom.* Oxford: Oxford University Press.

Laborde, C., 2010. Republicanism and global justice: a sketch. *European journal of political theory*, 9 (1), 48–69.

Laborde, C. and Maynor, J., eds., 2008a. *Republicanism and political theory.* Oxford: Blackwell.

Laborde, C. and Maynor, J., eds., 2008b. The republican contribution to contemporary political theory. *In*: C. Laborde and J. Maynor, eds. *Republicanism and political theory.* Oxford: Blackwell, 1–28.

Laborde, C. and Ronzoni, M., forthcoming. What is a free state? republican sovereignty, globalisation, and international justice.

Lovett, F., 2010. *A general theory of domination and justice.* Oxford: Oxford University Press.

Lovett, F. and Pettit, P., 2009. Neorepublicanism: a normative and institutional research program. *Annual review of political science*, 12 (1), 11–29.

McMahon, C., 2005. The indeterminacy of republican policy. *Philosophy and public affairs*, 33 (1), 67–93.

Miller, D., forthcoming. Is there a human right to immigrate? *In*: S. Fine and L. Ypi, eds. *Migration in political theory: the ethics of movement and membership.* Oxford: Oxford University Press.

Nabulsi, K., 1999. *Traditions of war: occupation, resistance, and the law.* Oxford: Oxford University Press.

Oberman, K., 2009. Immigration and freedom of movement. Thesis (DPhil). University of Oxford.

Oberman, K., forthcoming. Immigration as a human right. *In*: S. Fine and L. Ypi, eds. *Migration in political theory: the ethics of movement and membership.* Oxford: Oxford University Press.

Owen, D., 2009. Resident aliens, non-resident citizens and voting rights: towards a pluralist theory of transnational political equality and modes of political belonging. *In*: G. Calder, P. Cole and J. Seglow, eds. *Citizenship acquisition and national belonging: migration, membership and the liberal democratic state.* Palgrave -Macmillan: Basingstoke, 55–73.

Pettit, P., 1997. *Republicanism: A theory of freedom and government.* Oxford: Clarendon Press.

Pettit, P., 2001. *A theory of freedom: from the psychology to the politics of agency.* Oxford: Oxford University Press.

Pettit, P., 2002. Keeping republican freedom simple: on a difference with Quentin Skinner. *Political theory*, 30 (3), 339–356.

Pettit, P., 2008. Republican freedom: three axioms, four theorems. *In*: C. Laborde and J. Maynor, eds. *Republicanism and political theory.* Oxford: Blackwell, 102–130.

Pettit, P., 2010. A republican law of peoples. *European journal of political theory*, 9 (1), 70–94.

Sandel, M., 1996. *Democracy's discontent: America in search of a public philosophy*. Cambridge MA: Harvard University Press.

Skinner, Q., 1997. *Liberty before liberalism*. Cambridge: Cambridge University Press.

Skinner, Q., 2002. A third concept of liberty. *Proceedings of the British academy*, 117, 237–268.

Skinner, Q., 2008. Freedom as the absence of arbitrary power. *In*: C. Laborde and J. Maynor, eds. *Republicanism and political theory*. Oxford: Blackwell, 83–101.

Skinner, Q., 2010. On the slogans of republican political theory. *European journal of political theory*, 9 (1), 95–102.

Stilz, A., forthcoming. *Is there an unqualified right to leave? In*: S. Fine and L. Ypi, eds. *Migration in political theory: the ethics of movement and membership*. Oxford: Oxford University Press.

Walzer, M., 1983. *Spheres of justice: a defense of pluralism and equality*. New York: Basic Books.

Wellman, C.H., forthcoming. Freedom of movement and the rights to enter and exit. *In*: S. Fine and L. Ypi, eds. *Migration in political theory: the ethics of movement and membership*. Oxford: Oxford University Press.

Domination and migration: an alternative approach to the legitimacy of migration controls

Iseult Honohan

Politics and International Relations, University College Dublin, Dublin, Ireland

Freedom as non-domination provides a distinctive criterion for assessing the justifiability of migration controls, different from both freedom of movement and autonomy. Migration controls are dominating insofar as they threaten to coerce potential migrants. Both the general right of states to control migration, and the wide range of discretionary procedures prevalent in migration controls, render outsiders vulnerable to arbitrary power. While the extent and intensity of domination varies, it is sufficient under contemporary conditions of globalization to warrant limits on states' discretion with respect to admission. Reducing domination requires, rather than removing all immigration restrictions or democratically justifying them to all, that there be certain constraints on states' freedom to control migration: giving migrants a publicly secured status somewhat analogous to that enjoyed by citizens, subjecting migration controls to higher legal regulation, and making immigration policies and decision contestable by those who are subject to them.

Introduction

Whether states have the general right to exclude migrants is an issue that has been debated in terms both of freedom and of distributive justice. Here I address the issue of migration controls from the point of view of non-domination, a particular account of freedom that is broader than non-interference. Domination is understood as being subject to the arbitrary power of another in an unequal status relationship, and to the threat of coercion, whether or not there is actual interference at any particular point in time. This account of freedom has been articulated mainly at the domestic political level with respect to a bounded state, where it is understood to require certain kinds of institutional structures that guarantee and publicly recognize the equal status of citizens, provide for the contestability of decisions and protect citizens from arbitrary exercises of power. It is compatible with, and requires, extensive regulation by law, which, although it may interfere, does not dominate insofar as it is not arbitrary.

Migration is an area in which the theory of non-domination may seem to have particular relevance. While the classic cases of domination most frequently cited are slaves and wives within a patriarchal marriage, some of the starkest contemporary examples of vulnerability to arbitrary power may be seen in the realm of migration and access to citizenship, where states are considered to have a general right to determine entry and exclusion, and where broad discretionary procedures remain particularly widespread in practice. Those who are not fully protected by the legal structures, or are not participants in the political structures, of a state may be particularly vulnerable to the threat of domination. Non-citizens are vulnerable to domination by individuals and groups in society insofar as they lack the full range of protections of citizens, and by the state insofar as they lack the power to contest its decisions politically, and insofar as its powers over them are more discretionary than over citizens.

If we take non-domination as an important value to be realized, such domination of non-citizens has significant implications. The relevance of the theory seems clearly evident in the case of resident non-citizens. But here I address the more complex question of its application to controls on entry and residence. Non-domination provides a basis for considering migration controls that is different from other current arguments based on a right to free movement or on the need for coercion to be democratically justified.

I argue that the general power of states to exclude renders people vulnerable to domination by the state and by others. It applies not only to those who actually seek to enter, but also more widely, since the threat of interference or coercion hangs over all potential migrants. While it does not affect all equally, as the domination involved varies in intensity and extent, it is, especially under contemporary conditions of globalization, sufficiently intense to warrant limits on the freedom of states to control migration.

In contrast to an argument based on a right of free movement, reducing this domination does not require the lifting of immigration restrictions. It does require that potential immigrants gain something analogous, if not identical, to the publicly secured status that citizens enjoy. This means that states do not have complete discretion with respect to admission. Migration controls, to be non-dominating, need to be subject to a higher legal regulation, and policies and decisions need to be contestable by those who are subject to them.

The structure of the paper is as follows: the first section situates this argument in the context of some current discussions of freedom and migration controls. I then specify the conception of domination and non-domination applied here. After outlining the ways in which domination extends beyond the bounds of the state, I address the extent and intensity of domination exercised over outsiders by migration controls, and draw out some implications for constraints on the power of states to exclude. Before concluding, I respond briefly to the objection that constraining states' control of migration is itself dominating.

The impact of migration controls on freedom: recent arguments

In recent years a variety of arguments with respect to the impact of migration controls on freedom has emerged. It has been argued, most notably by Joseph Carens, that migration controls interfere with a right of freedom of movement (Carens 1987, 2014). But, if freedom of movement cannot be shown to be a right that warrants absolute constraints on others, can it the basis of a strong case against immigration controls? It can be argued that even if freedom of movement is an important interest, it may be limited in certain ways, and so does not constitute an absolute right (Miller 2005). It may be seen as needing to be balanced against other interests or rights (e.g. self-determination or free association) (e.g. Wellman 2008). Even if we accept free movement as a right, but one which is realizable only in an ideal world, it may not offer much in the way of guidance as to how we should address migration controls in our current non-ideal conditions (cf. Carens 1996).

A different argument, concerned with freedom as autonomy, and framed in the context of democratic theory, has been proposed by Arash Abizadeh, who claims that migration controls coerce all outsiders, and hence require some kind of democratic justification to all:

> a right to unilaterally control (and close) borders is incompatible with liberal and democratic reasons for the existence of borders (except under stringent circumstances) and [...] potential justifications for border restrictions must be addressed in democratic forums in which foreigners, on whom such restrictions coercively fall, also have standing to participate. (Abizadeh 2008, p. 54)[1]

But do migration controls in fact coerce all foreigners, or rather only *threaten* to coerce them, and thus do not require such justification? For David Miller, migration controls actually coerce only those who seek to enter or migrate to states, and coerce others at most hypothetically. In addition, they rule out only some options for those they exclude (who may be able to go to another country), thus *preventing* one action rather than coercing people into undertaking any specific action. Thus, he concludes, they do not invade autonomy in a way that requires democratic justification to all outsiders (Miller 2010).

If we accept that some people are more affected by migration controls than others, and that only some are actually coerced, the conclusion that the violation of autonomy they involve requires democratic justification to all may not be warranted. The democratic justification argument may not be a perfect fit for the threat to freedom constituted by migration controls. But even hypothetical coercion is not unproblematic, especially where there is more than a remote possibility that people may migrate. It is the problem of just such *threats of coercion*, wider than actual coercion, that the concept of domination grasps.

Accordingly, this exchange suggests that an examination of migration controls in the light of the conception of unfreedom as domination may provide some illumination. Recent theories of domination understand it in terms of the systematic threat of coercion, or vulnerability to the exercise of arbitrary power. If we can understand the danger to freedom that migration controls represent in terms of domination, this may lead to a conclusion with respect to such controls different from those reached by either Abizadeh or Miller.[2] In the rest of this article I examine whether migration controls dominate those outside the state, how serious is this domination and what implications can be drawn with respect to constraining the general right of states to control their borders.

It should be noted at this point that this argument does not depend on all being equally dominated by migration controls. Nor, as we shall see, is the problem of domination significantly addressed if other options remain, or if a state's migration controls prevent the uptake of only one option. Domination depends not only on the range of options available to a person, but also on the costs these involve, and the effect on their decision process with respect to any range of options.[3]

Domination and freedom as non-domination

The conception of domination invoked here has been developed by authors including Philip Pettit, Quentin Skinner and Frank Lovett (Pettit 1997a, 2001, Skinner 1998, 2008, Lovett 2010). Domination is understood as systematic subjection to the threat of interference even if one is not interfered with at a particular point in time. This theory thus identifies a broader range of situations of unfreedom than theories of freedom as non-interference.

To be dominated means to be systematically vulnerable to the exercise of arbitrary power in virtue of your status. Here the 'arbitrariness' of power is a matter of its being an unchecked exercise of the will of another, rather than its being 'random' or 'undeserved', as it is sometimes understood in moral debates. The classic examples of domination are those of a slave, or of a wife in a patriarchal marriage (Pettit 1997a, ch. 1). In both these cases, the person is unfree insofar as they are dependent on the good will of the master or husband. While the precise articulation of the nature of domination is a subject of internal debates among theorists of domination, I will adopt a recent formulation, in which it is usefully specified as follows: 'Persons or groups are subject to domination to the extent that they are dependent on a social relationship in which some other person or group wields arbitrary power over them' (Lovett 2010, p. 119). Thus, for the purposes of this argument I adopt a procedural account of the arbitrariness of domination in terms of will rather than interests.[4]

Domination thus arises in the context of some kind of relationship. Such relationships involve a form of interdependence, in which those exercising arbitrary power benefit from this, and those dominated either cannot leave the relationship, or exit costs are too high for them realistically to do so. Thus, domination exists (even in the absence of actual interference) wherever there is an unchecked capacity to interfere – or the *threat of coercion*.[5] This has constraining effects on the slave or wife; it affects their ability to live independent lives, and leads them to adjust their behaviour to ingratiate themselves with others in order to pre-empt interference. From this perspective, then, domination is broader than actual interference, and can be more pervasively damaging.[6]

Thus, the *threat* of coercion may constitute domination, a significant form of unfreedom that needs to be addressed. In contrast to some liberal or democratic approaches, what is at stake here is not the justification of coercion, but the reduction of domination. It is important to note also that since it is the arbitrariness rather than the interference that constitutes the harm of domination, it also means that not all interference is dominating, if it is subject to certain checks.[7]

It may be objected that domination is very pervasive, and thus not possible to address. But, against this, domination is a matter of degree; even if we cannot eliminate domination entirely, we may aim to reduce or minimize it. In contrast to some rights-based approaches, on this account freedom is not an all or nothing matter. Domination can vary in both intensity and extent. The intensity of domination depends on how arbitrary the interference can be, how easy it is for the dominator to interfere, and how severe are the measures that can be taken (Pettit 1997a, p. 58). The extent of domination depends on which areas of a person's life are subject to arbitrary interference, and the range of their options. The scope of domination, or how many people are affected, will also be relevant. For theorists of domination, the priority is identifying where there is domination and trying to intensify non-domination in those areas. This means that in promoting freedom on this view it is more important to constrain possibilities for arbitrary interference than to extend the range of choice. 'Reducing the intensity of domination is prior to increasing the range of choice' (Pettit 1997a, p. 106).

Freedom as non-domination

Non-domination, the kind of freedom that is promoted when domination is limited, is not a natural property, but has to be realized through certain kinds of institutional structures that guarantee and publicly recognize the equal status of citizens. These limit the capacity for arbitrary interference by creating a secure status for those who would otherwise be vulnerable to domination. Non-domination then is compatible with, and requires, extensive regulation by law, which, although it may interfere, does not dominate insofar as it is not arbitrary. There is, of course, a danger that the state itself may be dominating, if it rules in an arbitrary manner. So the legal and political structures that check power and protect against arbitrary interference (non-state and state) include more specifically:

(1) the rule of law and the publicly established equal status of citizens;
(2) accountable institutions in which power is dispersed; and
(3) the contestability of political decisions.

(1) The political implications of such a conception of freedom are a system of laws that provides guarantees against illegitimate interference, so that citizens may be able to act independently. On the non-domination view, freedom is not a condition that exists prior to law, nor an external consequence of the laws, but is constituted by the institutions of rights and accountability. By creating a recognized legal status that deters interference by others, these give immunity from interference rather like antibodies in the blood (Pettit 1997a, p. 108). It is arbitrary power, not law, that is incompatible with freedom. Laws provide security in non-interference, or resilient protection from domination. Freedom is a status, recognized by all, which receives institutional support. So the constraints of law are compatible with this (wider) status of freedom.

(2) To guard against the danger that the state may itself come to dominate, it is important that institutions be accountable. This supports the dispersal of power between different branches of government, a strong judiciary, and many kinds of appellate procedures to higher authorities with respect to acts of government. While not all actions of government can be specified precisely in law, the actions of government, agencies and officials in areas in which discretion is exercised can be framed by clear and transparent goals and principles that are publicly known, operate within guidelines for its use, and be subject to appeal and review, and to sanctions for abuse.[8]

(3) Rather than consent, ensuring the contestability of all decisions is the most important guideline for designing democratic institutions. In addition to institutional provision, this favours broad public debate and active social movements. These are required to give voice to all. 'Being a person is intimately tied up with enjoying a certain status in communion with others, and perhaps the best marker of the required status is that your voice is authorized by those others' (Pettit 1997b, p. 52).[9]

Those who are not citizens of states that secure their equal status through the rule of law, accountable institutions and contestable political decision-making processes are more vulnerable to domination. This can arise either where the state is not strong enough to protect against domination by others, or where the state's capacity to dominate is inadequately constrained. To the extent that contemporary constitutional democratic regimes provide a secure status of equality for citizens today, domination is tempered, but not eliminated. In other political regimes, the state may either dominate its citizens, or be too weak to protect them from domination by others. Relations of domination, moreover, are not confined within state boundaries.

Addressing domination – from domestic to global

While most domination theory so far has focused on tackling domination within the state, it is clear that arbitrary powers of interference extend beyond state boundaries. Both states and non-state actors can dominate citizens of other states to the extent that they have the power to interfere arbitrarily in their lives, where they lack institutions strong enough to protect them. This is evident in the case of those who are ruled by imperial or colonial powers. But domination arises also to the extent that people are subject to unconstrained powers which reach across state boundaries, whenever state power is not adequate to constrain these, and when there are no structures that work to minimize domination at an international level. These can be, for example, transnational corporations, international market actors or international agencies. Domination arises when ostensibly independent states are in dependent relationships with stronger states, or subject to arbitrary interference by international agencies. In the contemporary world even relatively successful liberal democratic states are not fully capable of protecting their citizens effectively from domination by such agents (Bohman 2007). It can be argued that globalization has involved an increase in the potential for domination, with increasing connectedness, asymmetry of power and dependence across borders (especially, but not exclusively, of those in less developed countries). It operates both directly on individuals, and indirectly by rendering their states incapable of fulfilling their protective role. Cécile Laborde and Miriam Ronzoni have argued that states (in particular, but not only, less developed states) are dominated by the institutions of globalization, which are shaped by the interests of wealthy powers and allow developed states and international corporations to require states, for example, to open up their markets, to concentrate on commodity production, to offer low tax rates, and to reduce pay levels and regulation of work conditions. 'Globalisation then, may be accused both of offering opportunities for some states to dominate others, and for powerful non-state actors to exercise some domination over all states, albeit not to the same degree' (Laborde and Ronzoni, forthcoming).

Thus, there has been some discussion among analysts of domination how to address such domination extending across borders. On one account, it means that there is a need for a multilevel global democracy (Bohman 2007) or a global republic (Marti 2010); on another, it means that we should aim to ensure that weaker states are better secured from domination (Maynor 2012, Laborde and Ronzoni, forthcoming).

What is agreed by all these authors is that domination extends across borders and beyond communities of citizens. While Laborde and Ronzoni focus on the problem of the domination of states, this affects individual citizens directly in a variety of ways. As Laborde puts it:

> Multifaceted processes of globalisation have meant that the geographical and symbolic superimposition of extremes of wealth and destitution have created new forms of status anxiety and despair, as the global poor become aware of their permanent reject status from an inaccessible but omnipresent rich world. (Laborde 2010, p. 52)

The question I address here is the extent to which migration controls, in creating different levels of reject status, contribute to situations of domination.

Migrants and domination

On the account of domination given so far, migration controls in the contemporary world are *prima facie* dominating. First of all, they are justified in terms of a general right of states to determine whom to admit and whom to exclude: this is arbitrary power to the extent that there are no, or very limited, international checks or accountability with respect to these, and those to whom they apply have an unequal status, and cannot contest the laws involved.[10] Moreover, the implementation of migration controls features a wider range and extent of discretionary powers, with fewer constraints, than prevail in domestic policy areas.[11]

The case may seem to be more easily established for the argument that, within the state, migrants or resident non-citizens are subject to domination. They clearly lack an equal status and the full range of protections of citizens; state powers over them are more discretionary than over citizens, they lack the power to contest decisions politically, they are dependent on the relationship with the host society and the state, and either cannot exit from this, or risk high costs of exit (Benton 2010, see also Benton, Fine and Hovdal-Moan 2014, all in this issue).

The focus of this article, however, is on those *outside* the state, who are potential or would-be migrants. I argue that, in a context of globalized relationships, if states are recognized as having a general right to exclude, migration controls are inherently dominating. Moreover, in practice, the more widely discretionary are the procedures through which these controls are implemented, the more dominating they may be in their effects.

It may be objected that, even if we understand the threat of coercion as domination, migration controls threaten to coerce only those with an immediate intent to migrate; others with no intent to migrate, are not dominated. Moreover, it may seem implausible to suggest that those in more developed countries are dominated by one another's controls. Thus, it might be denied that a citizen of the United States is dominated by Finnish migration controls. Yet domination is a matter of degree, where some are affected more than others;

some are subject to rather limited or weak domination by any single state. To warrant addressing domination politically, it is not necessary to show that all are equally dominated by migration controls. What is important is to establish how pervasive are their effects (Carens 2014, ch. 11), and whether they create a level of domination intense enough to warrant intervention.

To begin with, we should not underestimate the extent to which all non-citizens are subject to these controls (with the marginal exclusions of those who live in special travel areas or regional polities). If they want to enter or live in another country they will face the controls which that country places on movement, whether this be for purposes of transit, entering for a temporary period, gaining a work permit, living with their family, and so on. These apply to citizens of developed states as well as others, even if the controls vary for different categories of migrant, and may sometimes be waived for some. The impact of migration laws even on those in developed states is not negligible. Migration controls such as visa requirements and security clearance apply to them even if they do not plan to become long-term residents, and they too generally have no power to contest decisions.[12] Further, those who actually do apply and are rejected for admission or residence are dominated (to the extent that they lack a secure legal status, right of contestation of the laws or process, and often no right of appeal). But we may go further to say that those threatened with rejection are also dominated, including those who adapt their expectations to the reality of its difficulty, and who would be likely to apply for entry if they had greater expectation of success (Carens 2014). Thus, the domination of outsiders through migration controls extends beyond the *immediate* threat of coercion. We can agree, nonetheless, that not everyone will be equally dominated by migration controls; those who have satisfactory lives in their own countries, and who do not have reasons to migrate, whether economic, political, cultural or family-based, are less affected by these controls.

So, whether migration controls warrant constraint will depend on the intensity and extent of the domination they exercise over outsiders. We should acknowledge that someone in Asia is not subject to the continual threat of interference in their lives by Western states with strict migration controls in the same way as slaves or wives in the classic examples.[13] They do not live in daily fear of the impending exercise of the dominator's power over their every action, thus do not become instruments of the dominator's will in the same sense (cf. Miller 2010, p. 118). By comparison, non-citizen residents, and especially the illegal migrant or the visa overstayer, are more closely analogous to the wife or slave; in the light of their insecure status, they have to be wary of non-state actors such as employers and landlords, and of the possible incursion of state controls in police and other checks. Those outside the state cannot be seen as vulnerable to domination by migration controls in exactly the same way. We need then to examine more closely the intensity and extent of domination of outsiders that is entailed in migration controls.

The intensity and extent of domination by migration controls

The *intensity* of domination, as noted above, will depend on the degree of arbitrariness; the ease of exclusion; and the severity of the measures excluding foreigners (Pettit 1997a, p. 58). The intensity of domination of migration controls is then a function, first, of the general right (with limited exceptions) of states to decide who to admit and who to exclude. The arbitrariness of migration controls appears in the way in which the exact requirements for migration are liable to change according to the will of the admitting state; would-be migrants thus face frequently changing criteria for, for example, accepted labour skills, economic resources, and language and other requirements. The intensity is increased by the arbitrariness that arises from the greater prevalence of discretionary powers in the area of migration than in most areas of domestic policy: here agencies and officials are given wide powers, often laid down without legislative provision or oversight; their decisions are often not subject to review, judicial or otherwise; the framework within which they make decisions is often neither clearly laid out nor well known to citizens as well as non-citizens. As to the ease of exclusion, while states have difficulty in excluding migrants entirely, they can readily restrict legal access, and impose illegal status on those who breach entry controls; and they can shift the burden of controlling borders to others (other states, carriers, etc.). Finally the severity of the procedures, which (even when not discretionary in practice) range from exclusion by walls and barbed-wire fences, through deportation to detention or incarceration of illegal migrants. Even in the case of, for example, family reunification, where there are norms of more favourable treatment, the procedures can include stringent tests of language, and demanding requirements of financial resources. There is clear evidence of the dominating impact of these provisions on individuals – they lead people to change their behaviour in order to avoid coercive exclusion in ways that include destroying basic identity documents, marrying someone for whom they have no affection, leaving their families, learning (and speaking) other languages, and choosing or changing careers in the hope of facilitating mobility and gaining admission somewhere that will offer them better prospects of earning a living.[14]

The *extent* of domination will depend, first, on the range of areas of their lives affected, and the degree to which their options are limited for those who are excluded. On this basis, evidence suggests that the extent of domination by migration controls is significant. The whole lives of potential migrants who lack the basics of a reasonable level of subsistence may be determined by the difficulty of migration, which leaves them unable to access the preconditions for a flourishing life – even if they are not continuously subject to interference in each aspect of their lives. In cases where migration controls prevent spouses or parents with young children living together, this exclusion also affects a central area of their lives. For those who already have the basics, exclusion limits their options, and also constitutes domination (though this may be seen as less serious, since extending the range of options is less important than reducing the intensity of domination).[15]

The scope of domination will also depend in part on the numbers of people affected. Here we have seen that migration controls affect not just those who attempt to migrate, but the many who have significant reason to do so, whether political, economic, cultural, familial, or religious, or more specifically, where they might be able to move from countries where there is no level of secure non-domination, to a country where they might gain such security. A state's migration controls may also reinforce the capacity of other states to dominate their own citizens to the extent that they have no real option of leaving the country.

But it is not just the case that migration controls have intensive and extensive effects on many outsiders. What makes migration controls particularly dominating of potential migrants is that they are in *a relationship of dependence* with the countries which exclude them. In a global economy and society, potential migrants can be seen as living in a relationship of dependence, in which those exercising arbitrary power benefit, and those dominated either cannot leave the relationship, or their exit costs are too high for them to do so realistically. Drawing on the arguments of Laborde and Ronzoni, for example, we may argue that significant numbers of potential migrants are indeed in such a relationship with countries with strict migration controls; these countries benefit from a relationship which secures low-cost commodities and labour costs abroad, taxation advantages, etc. Moreover, this is a relationship from which would-be migrants cannot easily exit (in the absence of other countries to migrate to or other options for securing non-domination). Indeed, migration controls (and the associated sanctions) literally make individuals' exit from this dependency relation impossible or extremely costly.

Without such relations, in a world of genuinely independent states, the scope of domination through migration controls could perhaps be limited to the – still significant – numbers of those coerced or threatened with coercion, who actually sought and were refused entry, or who would have sought entry if there seemed a greater possibility of legal migration.[16] This latter should not be underestimated: a 2013 study reports that up to 90% of men aged 18–35 years surveyed in Senegal said they would migrate if they had the papers to do so.[17] In practice, under conditions of contemporary globalization, migration controls dominate in the context of those asymmetrical power relationships, in which people are dependent on, and subject to, the arbitrary power of corporations, wealthier states, international organizations and others. Moreover, while any individual state excludes would-be migrants only from its own state, in a world migration regime where all states have migration controls (albeit of varying stringency), it may be argued that there is a distributed system of domination, to which all states contribute in their migration decisions, even if no state can solely coerce a would-be migrant to do a particular thing, namely to stay in their own country.[18]

Thus, even if not all are equally dominated, migration controls constitute domination of sufficient intensity and extent to warrant addressing. We have seen that they have a major effect on the actions and lives of many of those excluded, especially in a context of relationships of dependence, and have effects that extend to a significant proportion of the world's population.[19]

If it is important to address domination that is significant in intensity and extent, we can draw the implications that the arbitrariness of migration controls should be limited.

An initial outline of what would be required to reduce domination in this context would include establishing the legal status of migrants, and recognizing their equality in respects other than admission; applying the rule of law to migration controls by limiting arbitrary powers and constraining discretionary procedures; making accountable the institutions determining migration law and policies by the introduction of a higher regulatory authority; and, finally, making migration laws and policies contestable in some way by those who are subjected to them. This does not mean that migration controls should be lifted entirely – domination does not mean the absence of interference, nor that they need to be democratically justified to all – domination requires restriction, not justification. This would not require global governmental institutions, but could be implemented through a competence-specific authority like the United Nations High Commissioner for Refugees (UNHCR), though with greater powers.[20] Contestation would not be limited to individual appeal on entry decisions, but also include the possibility of referring migration laws to an overseeing authority; yet the capacity to contest would not amount to full democratic justification, and what kind of, and how much, participation in decisions about migration law is entailed, is a question left open here.

This is a single-step approach to criticizing and modifying existing domination through migration regimes. This approach is not framed in terms of a distinction between the ideal and what can be hoped for in a non-ideal world. Domination is always a matter of degree, as people may be more or less dependent on a social relationship, and others may have more or less arbitrary power over them. Because non-domination is a goal to be pursued, and a matter of degree, rather than an absolute constraint on action, unlike, for example, a right of free movement may be understood, this has certain consequences. Compared with a right of free movement, it does not pose such a stark contrast between an ideal and a non-ideal situation. It does not frame the problem of migration controls in a way that distinguishes (say) between an ideal situation of maximum non-domination, and a non-ideal situation where we recognize the reality of domination, but attempt to temper its effects (cf. Carens 1996 and his critics). Being concerned with the reduction of domination wherever it appears, this approach can be applied critically to existing migration control regimes to identify those which dominate more intensely and to a greater extent, and various ways that this might be addressed, even if more is required to determine specific policies in different contexts.

An objection: regulating migration controls will dominate states

It may be objected at this point that there is a contradiction between the fundamental goal of non-domination and imposing constraints on the powers of states. If the freedom of citizens depends on a state to protect them from not only internal, but also external, domination, then states themselves must not be subject to external interference. On some views such constraints and oversight of states' migration laws and policies could themselves be seen as dominating (e.g. Fine 2014).[21]

The foundation for this view may be seen in republican political theory, the tradition in which contemporary non-domination theory has its clearest roots. On one influential account, republican non-domination rests on two planks: the free person and the free state. This has been expressed most clearly by Quentin Skinner, who identifies these as the two central axioms in the tradition: for it to be possible to act freely you must be a free person; and you can live and act freely only if you live in a free state (Skinner 2010, pp. 98–99). Thus, the freedom of the person is secured only in a state with internal protections against domination, and which itself is not subject to the threat of arbitrary interference from outside.

This raises large issues concerning the nature of states' freedom. Here I am concerned specifically with the suggestion that restricting states' right to exclude constitutes a form of domination.

The basis of the state's right may be expressed in terms either of the people's right to self government or of the sovereignty of the state itself. To be self-governing, it may be argued, a people must be able to determine who is and who is not accepted as a member, and that this extends to controlling entry. To respond briefly to these objections, I argue that a people may have a right to be self-determining, but this does not include a right to choose their members, in so far as a political community is not strictly analogous to a club, in which membership is a matter of consent, but rather a group of people whose membership stems from their being or becoming collectively subject to a common political authority.[22]

Even if we were to grant self-determining peoples the right to determine who their members are, control of membership is not the same as control of *territory*, and does not extend to controls on entry or general discretion in exclusion.[23] While a people may be justified in resisting domination by excluding invading forces or colonizing powers, this does not apply to migrants, who are not intrinsically dominators – insofar as they lack a superior status and are not in a position to exercise arbitrary power over the existing population.

A second formulation relies on the notion of state sovereignty, in seeing the free state as the guarantor of non-domination, so that over-ruling the state constitutes domination. On this point, it may be responded that, even if we accept that the state is sovereign in certain respects, sovereignty is composed of different elements, some more central than others. Control over borders is less central than the state's authority vis-à-vis its subjects and other states, and has not always been understood to be an essential part of sovereignty (Krasner 1999).

Furthermore, even if a 'free state' of some sort is necessary for non-domination, this does not mean that no constraints on that state's powers are justified. A free state is one that is not dominated, rather than a state that is not interfered with at all. Interventions that are not arbitrary may be justified. On this view the understanding of freedom as non-domination rather than non-interference would suggest a reformulation of the notion of sovereignty itself.[24]

If we agree that free states are essential to securing non-domination, but deny that this rules out all intervention in their affairs, we can see that regulating or limiting the right of states to control migration does not inherently undermine or contradict the promotion of non-domination.

Conclusion

I have argued that domination exercised through migration controls is of an intensity and extent to warrant limiting the discretionary power of states to grant or refuse admission. The non-domination approach offers a freedom-grounded critique that does not depend on an absolute or overriding right of freedom of movement, nor assume that all are equally coerced by migration controls and argue that they must accordingly be democratically justified to all.

It aims to reduce the most intense domination even if domination cannot be eliminated entirely. This does not mean abolishing migration controls; it does mean limiting the arbitrary power of states to exclude. In contrast to other, rights-based, arguments, reducing domination does not require the lifting of immigration restrictions, but that they should become less dominating. It does require that potential immigrants gain something analogous, if not identical, to the publicly secured status that citizens enjoy. This means that states do not have complete discretion with respect to admission. For migration controls to be less dominating, national immigration laws need to be less arbitrary, state policies and decisions to be subject to higher legal oversight, and discretionary procedures to be more constrained and contestable by those who are subject to them.

Acknowledgements

I would like to thank those who commented on earlier versions of this article presented at the 'Ethics and Immigration' conference at the European University Institute (EUI), Florence, May 2012; the participants in the Dublin Political Theory workshop; and the 'Immigration, Toleration and Nationalism' conference, in Helsinki, May 2013. Particular thanks are due to Kieran Oberman, Marit Hovdal-Moan and two reviewers for their helpful suggestions.

Notes

1. In a more succinct formulation, Abizadeh puts it: 'Border laws pose a unique problem because they inherently subject both citizens and foreigners to the state's exercise of power. This is why a liberal democracy does not legitimately enjoy absolute discretion to determine its own border laws: for the same reason that it does not have absolute discretion in how it treats its own domestic population' (Abizadeh 2012).
2. Autonomy is a more encompassing concept than non-domination; Miller and Abizadeh agree that it requires the capacity to form intentions, a sufficient range of valuable options and independence in choosing. Autonomy can be violated if any one of the three is absent (Abizadeh 2008, 2010, Miller 2010). Non-domination depends mainly on the third feature. The range of options is less central. Laborde and Ronzoni (forthcoming) distinguish domination and coercion on the basis that domination does not require actual coercion; that domination is not to be justified (as coercion) but minimized; that coercion does not necessarily dominate – only coercion that is arbitrary, i.e. not subject to control of those subject to it; and domination is by agents, but draws on systemic positions in society, while coercion may not.
3. Defeating the autonomy argument also relies on the availability of other options when one state excludes. How far this is a reality under current migration regimes is a matter of debate, and is addressed briefly below.
4. Issues arise with respect to whether the arbitrariness of domination rests in the exercise of will or the failure to track the interests of those affected; both were implied in Pettit's original formulation; the latter is problematical with respect to whether interests are to be understood subjectively or objectively. Differences also arise with respect to the nature of the procedural checks, and whether external constraints or more or less democratic contestation or both are essential to check domination. I see these as less significant differences within the broader account of domination as arbitrary interference in a relationship, where both external constraints and contestation by those affected may be required to reduce domination. There are other conceptual differences and unresolved issues within the conceptual debate on domination that I largely set aside here.
5. Note that this is a matter of capacity rather than likelihood (congruent with arbitrariness being a matter of will rather than unpredictability).
6. Being a matter of the threat of interference, however, it is not entirely separate from interference, and thus remains in most respects a negative conception of freedom.
7. Pettit also makes the distinction between what 'compromises' and what 'conditions' freedom, or more recently between what 'invades' and what 'vitiates' freedom (Pettit 2001, 2012).
8. By 'discretionary power' I understand power exercised according to an agent's decision rather than being completely specified in law. Not all discretionary power is arbitrary, however, and not all discretionary powers can or should be eliminated, as they can be essential for implementing general provisions in specific cases. For Lovett, justified discretion involves powers being exercised in the pursuit of commonly known goals, subject to oversight by those from whom they have been delegated, and with limits on their exercise (Lovett 2010, pp. 95–97, 217). Discretionary powers become arbitrary when they do not meet these criteria. See also Pettit (2013): in criticizing defences offered for the police treatment of David Miranda, Pettit argues for tight constraints on the occasions when special powers can be used, exact specification of how they can be used, effective channels of complaint for those affected, independent reviews of the ways in which the powers are used and sanctions for deviant officials.

9. How substantial are the democratic procedures that this requires is internally debated among theorists of domination (e.g. Pettit 1997b, Honohan 2002, Maynor 2003).
10. Insofar as the entry of refugees is an exception, this represents a limit in principle on the discretion of states to exclude.
11. Migration policies risk arbitrariness at two levels, since states are considered to have the right to determine their migration laws and policies independently of any other authority, and immigration procedures frequently involve determinations based on administrative decisions rather than by law.
12. Thus, when many work for international corporations, even a privileged person's promotion – or continuing job prospects – may depend on accepting a posting with their company in another country, and not happening to fall into a category restricted by that country's migration laws.
13. Family reunification of spouses and young children could be seen as one possible exception here.
14. A graphic fictional account of the ways in which people are willing to alter their behaviour in order to gain access to Western states features in Kiran Desai's *The Inheritance of Loss* (Desai 2006, pp. 182–187).
15. As Fine notes: 'Prohibiting outsiders from settling in and becoming members of a particular state hinders or prevents their pursuit of all the many familial, social, religious, cultural, political, or economic interests tied to residence and citizenship in that state, despite the fact that some, if not all, of their basic needs could be met elsewhere' (Fine 2010, p. 348).
16. This would be true even if those states were unequal in many respects, and even if many states did not do a good job of promoting non-domination internally – at least and only as long as domination of unrelated others by others is not considered to require action
17. A study of 8,000 people in 16 different areas within Morocco, Senegal, Turkey and Ukraine in 2011 shows that, in the age group 18–35 years, between 25% and 76% of women and between 43% and 90% of men aspired to emigrate in the next five years, with significantly higher percentages saying they would do so if they were given the papers. In Senegal these figures were highest: up to 65% of women and 94% of men would travel if they had the papers (Carling 2013).
18. Cf. Christiano (2008, p. 8) for a similar argument on the collective effects of individual states' migration policies. This addresses the objection that migration controls do not *coerce* anyone into doing a particular thing, but only *prevent* them doing one specific thing – namely, immigrate into that state's territory (Miller 2010). Miller recognizes that when many states collectively create a system of exclusion, or when they independently exclude where they have a responsibility to avoid restricting freedom, the result is more serious (Miller 2010, p. 118).
19. In the context of global relationships, the problem cannot wholly be addressed by attempting to reduce domination in migrants' own country as an alternative to reducing the domination of migration controls. Such an argument would parallel that for improving conditions in less developed states, making greater transfers of aid from better-off to less developed countries, sometimes proposed as an alternative to reducing migration controls in distributive justice arguments.
20. This is similar to the suggestion with respect to other policies put forward by Ronzoni in her argument for re-envisaging sovereignty (Ronzoni 2009, 2012).
21. Thus, Laborde and Ronzoni also argue that minimizing domination should focus on strengthening the capacity of states to protect their citizens rather than attempting to promote non-domination from the top down in global terms (Laborde and Ronzoni, forthcoming).

22. 'In the absence of full control over access to membership, a group still can be self-determining to the extent that it is free to set its own internal policy agenda without external interference. That freedom might be limited by the lack of control over membership rules, but liberal and democratic principles already constrain the extent of the citizens' discretion to control the membership of their political community' (Fine 2010, p. 353).
23. 'The citizens' collective right to freedom of association could not support a right to prevent outsiders crossing the state's borders anyway because their mere presence has no bearing on the citizens' individual or collective associational freedoms' (Fine 2010, p. 352). Some control on entry might be justified if migration was such as to undermine the very possibility of self-government (cf. Bauböck 2009; see also Bertram in this issue).
24. Cf. Ronzoni (2012), in which global regulatory institutions are seen as supporting rather than undermining positive sovereignty (see also Oberman, forthcoming, and others).

Notes on contributor

Iseult Honohan is Senior Lecturer in the School of Politics and International Relations, University College Dublin. Her research interests lie in republican thought and its applications to areas including migration and citizenship. Her publications include *Civic republicanism* (Routledge, 2002). She is a partner in EUDO Citizenship, the Citizenship strand of the European Union Observatory on Democracy.

References

Abizadeh, A., 2008. Democratic theory and border coercion: no right to unilaterally control your own borders. *Political theory*, 36 (1), 37–65.

Abizadeh, A., 2010. Democratic legitimacy and state coercion: a reply to David Miller. *Political theory*, 38 (1), 121–130.

Abizadeh, A., 2012. http://www.bostonreview.net/forum/case-amnesty/if-moral-duties-apply-domestic-noncitizens-they-apply-all-noncitizens-arash-abizadeh. Accessed 23 August 2013.

Bauböck, R., 2009. Global justice, freedom of movement and democratic citizenship. *European journal of sociology*, 50 (01), 1–31.

Benton, M., 2010. The tyranny of the enfranchised majority?' The accountability of states to their non-citizen population. *Res publica*, 16 (4), 397–413.

Benton, M., 2014. The problem of denizenship: a non-domination framework. *Critical review of international social and political philosophy*, 17 (1), 49–69.

Bohman, J., 2007. *Democracy across borders: from demos to demoi.* Cambridge, MA: MIT Press.

Carens, J., 1987. Aliens and citizens: the case for open borders. *Review of politics*, 49 (02), 251–273.

Carens, J., 1996. Realistic and idealistic approaches to the ethics of migration. *International review of migration*, 30 (1), 156–170.

Carens, J., 2014. *The ethics of immigration.* Oxford: Oxford University Press.

Carling, J., 2013. *Who wants to go to Europe? PRIO Policy Brief 4–2013: Results from a large-scale survey on migration aspirations.* PRIO: Oslo.

Christiano, T., 2008. Immigration, political community, and cosmopolitanism. *University of San Diego law review*, 45 (4), 933–961.

Desai, K., 2006. *The inheritance of loss.* London: Penguin.

Fine, S., 2010. Freedom of association is not the answer. *Ethics*, 120 (2), 338–356.

Fine, S., 2014. Non-domination and the ethics of migration. *Critical review of international social and political philosophy*, 17 (1), 10–30.

Honohan, I., 2002. *Civic republicanism*. Abingdon and New York: Routledge.

Hovdal-Moan, M., 2014. Unequal residence statuses and the ideal of non-domination. *Critical review of social and political philosophy*, 17 (1), 70–89.

Krasner, S., 1999. *Sovereignty: organized hypocrisy*. Princeton, NJ: Princeton University Press.

Laborde, C., 2010. Republicanism and global justice: a sketch. *European journal of political theory*, 9 (1), 48–69.

Laborde, C. and Ronzoni, M., forthcoming. What is a free state? A republican account of sovereignty and international justice.

Lovett, F., 2010. *A general theory of domination*. Oxford: Oxford University Press.

Marti, J.L., 2010. A global republic to prevent global domination. *DIACRÍTICA*, 24 (2), 31–72.

Maynor, J., 2003. *Republicanism in the modern world*. Oxford: Polity.

Maynor, J., 2012. Should republican liberty as non-domination be outsourced? Available at SSRN: http://ssrn.com/abstract=2134490 or http://dx.doi.org/10.2139/ssrn.2134490 (Accessed 2 Nov 2102).

Miller, D., 2005. *Immigration: the case for limits*. *In*: A.I. Cohen and C.H. Wellman eds. *Contemporary debates in applied ethics*. Oxford: Blackwell.

Miller, D., 2010. Why immigration controls are not coercive: a reply to Arash Abizadeh., *Political theory*, 38 (1), 111–120.

Oberman, K.forthcoming. Immigration as a human right. Available at. SSRN: http://ssrn.com/abstract=2164939 or http://dx.doi.org/10.2139/ssrn.2164939

Pettit, P., 1997a. *Republicanism*. Oxford: Oxford University Press.

Pettit, P., 1997b. Freedom with honor. *Social research*, 64 (1), 52–75.

Pettit, P., 2001. *A theory of freedom: from the psychology to the politics of agency*. New York: Oxford University Press.

Pettit, P., 2012. *On the people's terms: a republican theory and model of democracy*. Cambridge University Press.

Pettit, P., 2013. The police protect us, but occasionally we also need to be protected from them. *Irish times 25* August 2013 http://www.irishtimes.com/news/world/uk/the-police-protect-us-but-occasionally-we-also-need-to-be-protected-from-them-1.1503912. Accessed 11 September 2013.

Ronzoni, M., 2009. The global order: a case of background injustice? *Philosophy and public affairs*, 37 (3), 229–256.

Ronzoni, M., 2012. Two conceptions of state sovereignty and their implications for global institutional design. *Critical review of social and political philosophy*, 15 (5), 573–591.

Skinner, Q., 1998. *Liberty before liberalism*. Cambridge: Cambridge University Press.

Skinner, Q., 2008. Freedom as the absence of arbitrary power. *In*: C. Laborde and J. Maynor, eds. *Republicanism and political theory*. Oxford: Blackwell, pp., 83–101.

Skinner, Q. 2010. On the slogans of republican political theory, *European journal of political theory*, 95 (9), 95–102.

Wellman, C.H., 2008. Immigration and freedom of association. *Ethics*, 119 (1), 109–141.

The problem of denizenship: a non-domination framework

Meghan Benton

Migration Policy Institute, Washington, DC, USA

The status of being a non-citizen or 'denizen' has been described as second-class citizenship. But many instances of denizenship are not morally troubling, e.g. highly skilled temporary workers. This paper examines the conditions under which denizenship is problematic by developing a framework for addressing the problem of denizenship, structured around the republican ideal of non-domination. Denizens are subject to the coercive power of the state like citizens, but lack many of the accountability mechanisms citizens enjoy. Whether this matters, I argue, depends on their exit costs of leaving the state of denizenship: either by leaving the country or by acquiring citizenship. This model could inform policies in three areas: improving the accountability of countries to their non-citizen population, empowering denizens in private relationships and reducing arbitrariness in citizenship acquisition. Although republicanism provides the conceptual architecture for this study, the concept of 'exit costs' has wider relevance for immigration theory.

Introduction

The concept of non-domination – freedom from arbitrary or unchecked power – is central to modern republican thought. It is often identified with, and described as equivalent to, citizenship, as captured in the classic republican adage: 'to be free is to be citizen of a free state'. Like citizenship, non-domination has been described as a status of mutually acknowledged equality, autonomy and reciprocal power, exemplified by the ability to look your fellow citizens in the eye. It entitles and enables you to plan your life, secure in the knowledge that the state power you are subject to will not be abused, and that the power of your fellow citizens will be monitored and checked by legal constraints. An equivalent association exists between domination and subordination or second-class status. In fact, being dominated is described by one of the main champions of republican political thought, Philip Pettit (1997, p. 87), as the sense of having 'an inferior social status'.

Republicans are thus implicitly preoccupied with second-class citizenship. But to date they have said little about 'denizenship', or the status of being a resident non-citizen, despite the fact that (analytically at least) it epitomizes second-class status. For republicans, citizens rather than individuals are the appropriate beneficiaries of non-domination, just as the appropriate arena for the pursuit of non-domination is the bounded state.[1] This is surprising for two reasons. First, superficially at least, numerous aspects of the migrant experience resonate with some of the most frequently cited examples of domination. For example, unauthorized workers who fear deportation might do all they can to 'curry favour' with employers; women dependent on their husbands for the right to stay in a country might find themselves unable to leave abusive marriages; and migrants with limited entitlement to public services might become dependent on private charity. Second, it has long been noted that the existence of a disenfranchised populace of non-citizens looks a lot like *political* domination (e.g. Walzer 1983, Bauböck 1994, Shapiro and Hacker-Cordón 1999, Bohman 2007). Since denizens are subjects rather than citizens of their country of residence, their existence is inherently troubling to democrats and those suspicious of hierarchical or caste-like systems.

But the intuition that denizenship is tantamount to domination seems blunt or over-inclusive – one reason republicans may have steered clear of this debate. Many cases of subjecthood or non-citizenship are not intuitively troubling, such as a highly skilled temporary worker who lacks voting rights in her country of residence, but intends to return home in the near future.[2] This paper attempts to develop an alternative framework for addressing the problem of denizenship that accommodates these nuances. The first part outlines a conception of domination as *dependence on unaccountable power*; I go on in the second part to apply this framework to denizens and subgroups of denizens; in the third part I make the case for according equal weight to the non-domination of denizens and citizens; and finally, I identify areas where non-domination could inform policy.

My central argument is that denizens are vulnerable to domination if they are subject to power insufficiently checked by accountability mechanisms, and if their costs of exit from the status of denizenship (either by leaving the country or by acquiring citizenship) are high. These costs of exit derive from personal circumstances (such as, for example, personal ties and work in the host country or fear of persecution in the country of origin) combined with institutional factors (such as naturalization laws). While republicanism provides the conceptual architecture for this study, the findings – and specifically my analysis of the costs of exit from the state of denizenship – may inform immigration theory more broadly.

Freedom as 'non-domination'

Recent years have seen a great deal of interest in reviving republican political theory, an ideology with a long heritage tracing back to Roman jurisprudence.

The cornerstone of this tradition is a particular theory of liberty: freedom as non-domination. According to this school of thought, people are free if they live in a society where institutions are designed to ward against the abuse of power, they have an equal status with their peers, and the laws to which they are subject are set out and applied in an even-handed way. In other words, they need to be resiliently independent from arbitrary power.

Freedom as non-domination is distinguished from the more mainstream conception of freedom as non-interference by its emphasis on how power relations can curb freedom, regardless of whether there is interference. Theorists of non-domination contend that interference, while *generally* limiting freedom, does not do so *necessarily*. Some interference – such as a well-promulgated law in the common interest – can promote rather than impede freedom. For example, laws against violence promote freedom by providing people with security against the interference of others (Laborde and Maynor 2008, p. 8).

A person can also be unfree in the absence of interference if someone has an unchecked power to interfere with her at any time. For example, a slave with a lazy or benevolent slave master is still a slave, even if she has considerable latitude to make certain choices. Even a slave with a draconian master can learn to abstain from behaviour that tends to incur his wrath; while such a slave might avoid interference, she is not 'more free' than one who has not (Lovett 2006). Similarly, a subject of a benevolent dictatorship might live in fear of what will happen if the dictator's mood changes or his evil brother inherits power. In the former case, the risk is of abuse of private power (*dominium*, in the republican lingo), and in the latter of state power (*imperium*). With both sorts of power, the mere possibility of arbitrary interference not only makes people less free in a philosophical sense – it is also likely to make them *feel* less free.

While philosophers from Machiavelli to Milton have been described as early advocates of this theory, the lion's share of the conceptual work is recent (e.g. Pettit 1997, Skinner 1997, Lovett 2010). According to Pettit's seminal work on domination, someone has dominating power over me if they can interfere with me arbitrarily, without being 'forced to track [my] interests'.[3] In the remainder of this section, I propose three modifications to Pettit's theory of freedom.

From 'arbitrariness' to 'accountability gaps'

Arbitrariness – and Pettit's understanding of it – has proved one of the thorniest elements of republican freedom. A common criticism is that it implies freedom is limited only by interference that is not in the interests of the person being interfered with (Carter 2008). This undermines republican freedom's credentials as a form of negative liberty since it implies that people need only to be free from sort of interference from which they *should* be free. It follows – on this line of attack – that republicans are basing their theory of freedom on a value judgment about 'good' and 'bad' types of interference, which falls foul of the classic objection to positive liberty that it could justify forcing people to be free.

While this is objection is compelling, it does not ultimately succeed. As Pettit makes clear, what matters is that the power-holder is *forced* to track the interests, not that interference happens to result in someone's interests being promoted. The eventual alignment of outcomes and interests is irrelevant to its arbitrariness. Another way of putting this is that rather than asking whether the quality of interference is such that it is in someone's interests, we should determine whether adequate mechanisms exist to *ask* whether power is being exercised in someone's interests.

In my model of republican freedom, 'non-arbitrariness' is fleshed out as 'institutional accountability', defined as the responsiveness of institutions or agents to the interests of those subject to their power (Benton 2010). This substantiates, rather than deviates from, standard republican theory, since replacing the 'controls' dimension of arbitrariness with accountability is in line with statements made by most republican theorists. Accountability is a near-antonym of impunity, which itself is almost universally emphasized as a component of domination (e.g. Skinner 2008). But since accountability lacks the all-or-nothing character of impunity, I propose we seek to identify accountability gaps. These exist, on my account, when there are insufficient checking mechanisms that require that state power is justified to all subjects of the power (justification), that subjects of the power are able to complain if their interests are not being met (contestation), and that power-holders are duly punished if they fail to track the interests of power-subjects (retribution). Accountability mechanisms can be seen as systemic questions asked of the exercise of power in order that it be used in the right way: a way that tracks interests. While it is the existence of the questions rather than a positive answer to them that makes power non-arbitrary, if accountability crosses a certain threshold, non-domination will obtain; below that threshold domination will obtain.

While philosophers might disagree about exactly where this threshold is, these three types of checks nonetheless allow us to make comparative judgements about different cases. We can take any instance of state power, from detention to taxation, and assess what accountability mechanisms exist. This model allows us to say, for example, that citizens of North Korea are clearly subject to greater unaccountable power than citizens of the United Kingdom. Alternatively, we can make comparisons between different groups of people. Unauthorized immigrants clearly have fewer accountability mechanisms at their disposal if they are detained than permanent residents.

From 'subjection' to 'dependence'

My second departure from the dominant theory of non-domination is the addition of dependence as a component of domination. On Pettit's view, subjection to arbitrary power is a sufficient criterion for domination to obtain. But, as Frank Lovett (2010) forcefully argues, it is surely worse to be in a situation of domination from which you cannot extricate yourself than one where you are free to leave; indeed, it makes sense to describe the former as 'more dominating'. According to Lovett, dependence is not dominating of itself – indeed we consider many dependent relationships to be valuable – but it amplifies domination wherever it exists. This addition is helpful since it shows both why levels of private domination increase where people are unable to leave the relationship, and also why being able to leave a *society* can affect domination in both its private (*dominium*) and state (*imperium*) forms.

To see this, consider a woman in an abusive marriage. Clearly, she is more vulnerable to domination (*dominium*) in a society that outlaws divorce than one that permits it, since she could not leave her marriage. Analogously, citizens of a country they are prevented from emigrating are more vulnerable to abuses of state power or *imperium* than citizens of a society with no restrictions on exit. But these two factors in combination yield higher levels of domination than they do independently; women are more vulnerable to domination at the hands of their husbands if they cannot escape the institutional framework that prohibits divorce. The next section, on the domination of denizens, will illustrate this distinction further.

With Lovett, I define dependence as the subjective exit costs of leaving a relationship. My contention is that someone is dominated if their costs of exit from an unaccountable power relationship – one unchecked by one or more of the accountability mechanisms – are high.

Group domination

The final adjustment flows from the previous addition of dependence as a condition of domination. According to Pettit (1997, pp. 122–123), membership of a group alone can make you dominated. Women and ethnic minorities are 'vulnerability classes', meaning that if you are a woman or a member of an ethnic minority, 'to the extent that they are dominated, you too are dominated' and 'to the extent that any woman can be abused on an arbitrary basis by her husband, womanhood is a badge of vulnerability'. The claim that all women in a patriarchal society are equally dominated seems a drastic one. Indeed, it contradicts other statements Pettit makes, including one to the effect that internal differences may arise since members 'may be well situated relative to other members' and 'do slightly better in the protections that are available to them'. Since this paper addresses the question of group (i.e. denizen) domination, the issue of whether someone can be dominated merely by virtue of membership of a status is pertinent.

A potential resolution to this paradox is that individual domination levels vary, but *vulnerability* to domination is shared. According to the definition set out above, domination is likely to be the result of more than group membership.

Meanwhile, some people may be members of multiple vulnerability classes – ethnic minority women, for example. Shared vulnerability could derive from a structural feature of group membership that indicates an increase or decrease in the relative components of domination, even while actual levels of domination vary.

One such shared structural feature of group membership is dependence. Since the shared feature of the vulnerability classes Pettit cites is that the group is impossible to leave, it is in the interests of women to improve their group rather than individual status. This approach emphasizes the fact that freedom is shared, collective, and only resiliently guaranteed by one's status. Women cannot leave the group of women, thus womanhood is a 'badge of vulnerability' (Pettit 1997, p. 123). Whether denizens are – like women – dependent on the status of womanhood, is therefore a fruitful line of inquiry for the next section.

Denizens and domination

The modified definition of domination as dependence on unaccountable power outlined above establishes a clear set of criteria for determining whether denizens are susceptible to domination. It proposes we consider: (1) the kinds of state and private power to which denizens might be subject; (2) whether this power is subject to accountability mechanisms; and (3) whether denizens are dependent on these power relationships. Because state power is more universally distributed, I turn to that first.

Arbitrary power

Since governments can interfere with only those who are citizens in rather few ways – e.g. conscription, jury service and voting – denizens also are subject to the vast power of the state over taxation, legislation and coercion.[4] The state also has special powers over denizens alone, namely the capacity to transform the status of denizens either through detention and deportation (in essence, forcibly transforming non-citizen residents into non-citizen non-residents). Hence, theoretically, denizens are subject to a greater level of *imperium* than citizens.

That this power is arbitrary might be thought to be fairly straightforward. Politicians lack the electoral incentive to promote the interests of their non-citizen population if these lack voting rights. Even if human rights (and, by extension, rights held by denizens) are constitutionally protected, everyday policy-making is likely to be skewed in favour of the citizen majority (Bellamy 2007, Benton 2010). That said, matters are rarely as clear-cut as democratic theory predicts. The executive is held to account by its wider political party, as well as by parliamentary committees and opposition parties; representatives have good reason to work for their non-citizen constituents either as potential future voters or to court family or community members who can vote. Membership of a wider ethnic or national group can be the source of political capital, as demonstrated recently by the mobilization of political support (in order to court the 'Hispanic vote') for legalizing unauthorized workers in the United States. Meanwhile, the interests of non-citizens may be promoted by ethnic or religious groups or pressure groups, and by employment unions. Thus, the distinction between the political power of those eligible and ineligible to vote may not be as stark as it seems.

The democratic accountability gap might equally be filled by protections that derive from one's country of citizenship, such as diplomatic protection. Bauböck (2009) has referred to these extraterritorial rights and privileges as 'external citizenship'. But here, clear differences emerge depending on denizens' citizenship status and country of citizenship. At the extreme, refugees and stateless persons are wholly excluded from the privileges of external citizenship. For others, their country of origin shapes the character and forcefulness of diplomatic protection. While countries having political ties or bilateral agreements with countries that are home to their migrant diaspora might be more able to intervene, e.g. by providing legal assistance and mediating in labour disputes, others might be unwilling to jeopardize economic gains if they rely on foreign aid and migrant remittances. Those with a powerful international presence may be better able to intervene in the protection of their citizens than countries with weaker international clout. Finally, the integrity of diplomatic protection as an accountability mechanism depends on whether their political institutions force home countries to be responsive to the interests of their 'ex-pats'. Citizens of democracies enjoy greater external protection than those from dictatorships, but even democracies sometimes disenfranchise their citizens after a period of non-residence.

Dependence on state power

According to my framework, unaccountable power is dominating when exit is costly. I suggested above that lack of an exit option from certain forms of group membership such as minority status or womanhood might explain why these have, at times, functioned as second-class statuses. Unlike these minority groups, denizens have two separate exit routes at their disposal.

Leaving denizenship can mean either leaving the country entirely, or leaving the state of denizenship, in other words becoming a citizen. This insight helps unpick a basic intuition about denizenship. High exit costs of leaving a country would be less troubling if you could easily naturalize, i.e. transform your status from one of domination. The dependence of denizens on denizenship (a state of unaccountable power) can therefore be characterized as the sum total of the exit costs of leaving the state and leaving the state of denizenship.

Unlike subjection to arbitrary power, the cost to denizens of leaving both the state and the status of denizenship vary considerably. One especially important dimension is that the cost of returning to one's home country will be prohibitively high for refugees or people who have left countries with high levels of civil unrest, or for those with special medical needs such as HIV-positive status. For these groups, returning home may not even be an option. Exit costs of emigrating – for citizens and denizens alike – depend on both the viability of a life elsewhere and the relative costs of leaving. Social networks, employment opportunities and special connections elsewhere, including citizenship of another state, may be offset against opportunities and commitments in one's state of residence, including relationships, networks, health care, educational involvements and long-term contracts such as mortgages.[5] In addition, these costs can affect people in different ways. For those living on the bread line, returning home or moving elsewhere may be financially prohibitive; others might retain debts to smugglers or family members. Emotional costs are clearly more subjective – some people find it easy to live in different countries as they adopt a cosmopolitan approach to new cultures; others are more risk averse in this respect.

For many residents, the costs of leaving the state are likely to increase just as the costs of acquiring citizenship diminish. Most destination countries stipulate minimum residency periods before naturalization can occur, along with requirements ranging from language proficiency to a clean criminal record to fulfilment of citizenship courses or tests (e.g. Hampshire 2009, Seglow 2009). All else being equal, as time passes we expect individuals to develop deeper ties to their country of residence and find it more difficult to leave.[6] Meanwhile, they move closer to the minimum length of residence required to acquire citizenship, and (theoretically at least) find it easier to fulfil many of the other requirements of naturalization such as language proficiency. This provides support for the view, shared by many immigration scholars, that length of residence strengthens an individual's moral claim on their country of residence.

But this relationship will not always be straightforward. Naturalization – in principle carrying the same cost for everyone – may translate into different subjective costs in practice. Financial costs may be prohibitively expensive for some but not for others, while having to give up citizenship of one's home country may rule out naturalization for some, yet be merely trifling for others. A further problem is that some groups of denizens are effectively debarred from the acquisition of citizenship. Unauthorized migrants have no easy exit from their status, and even those who are eligible for legalization may find it difficult to prove continued residence for the required number of years (because of an absence of official documentation that other workers take for granted). Similarly, requirements such as a clean criminal record can preclude naturalization.

Private power

What makes the vulnerability of denizens to domination so different is the way that these exit costs of leaving the country can interact with *private* forms of power. For denizens who lack the right to stay in the country, high exit costs of leaving the country can exacerbate dependence on private relationships with employers or family members. Consider a woman on a visa 'that requires she stay married' for her right to remain in the country, or a worker whose right to stay is contingent on remaining with a particular employer. These cases are intuitively troubling for the way that they tie someone to a particular power relationship. But if we add in the additional dimension, that someone may face very high exit costs of emigrating, we can see how the domination of the private relationship appears to increase. Dependence on staying in the country can thus contribute to dependence on private relationships, and by extension, to domination.[7] The converse is also true, that to the extent that a migrant can easily leave the country, visas that impose these sorts of conditions appear less problematic.[8]

A related point is that high exit costs of leaving the country contribute to the capacity for private individuals, including landlords or employers, to threaten deportation. Of course, this power is most acute with respect to unauthorized workers, where employers (like state officials) wield large amounts of power over their continued residence in the country. These migrants may avoid reporting crimes committed against them, for instance, for fear of alerting the authorities to their status. But even for those for whom deportation is a low risk may see their continued residence as conditional, and be disinclined to rock the boat. Thus, the state's transformative power over the status of migrants (as set out above) is reflected and to some extent shared by citizens of that state.

Vulnerability indicators

On the basis of this analysis, we can compile a list of factors that contribute to vulnerability to domination, or 'vulnerability indicators':

- *Immigration status*. Different types of visas facilitate different relationships of power and dependence. Unauthorized migrants are highly vulnerable to domination because each individual with whom they come into contact enjoys power over their status, through the threat of denunciation to the authorities. Meanwhile, visas that tie a migrant to a particular employment or personal relationship increase dependence to the degree that a migrant has high exit costs of leaving the country.
- *Country of origin*. Levels of both accountability and dependence vary with country of origin. European Union citizens enjoy strong accountability mechanisms, such as the protection of European Union institutions, local political rights and European courts. Likewise, citizens of countries with considerable international clout occupy a relatively favourable situation. By contrast, migrants from countries that benefit from migration or who have little diplomatic influence are more

vulnerable, as are, of course, refugees, who lack the protection of a state at all. Those who fear returning to their home country due to civil unrest, famine, poverty or persecution are likely to perceive their exist costs as much higher than others.

- *Length of residence.* All else being equal, length of residence is likely to correlate with the level of exit costs of leaving the country. Long-standing residents may be expected to be more vulnerable to domination. But, generally, exit from denizenship to citizenship becomes easier as exit from the country becomes harder – thereby allaying some of these concerns.
- *Wealth.* Richer migrants have significantly more political influence, both because states wish to attract and keep them and because they can wield political influence. Their dependence on the state is likely to be lower as they can afford the cost of migration elsewhere. Additionally, they are much less likely to be dependent on exploitative employment relationships.
- *Language, skills and education.* Those who understand the system and are able to speak the language are likely to be less vulnerable to domination. Additionally, workers with desirable skills enjoy favourable entry routes to many countries, hence high dependence on private relationships is unlikely to translate to considerable vulnerability to domination. By contrast, unskilled workers possess weaker bargaining power; they may find themselves highly dependent on exploitative employers or industries for a job.

In sum, as length of residence increases, the accountability gap for all non-citizens becomes more problematic, because dependence increases. But, to the extent that length of residence may also reduce the dependence on denizenship (because it makes access to citizenship easier), dependence overall will remain fairly constant. Therefore, under the right conditions, denizenship need not constitute domination. In addition, within the group of 'denizens' (like the group of 'women') there is considerable variation in levels of subjection to domination. But since denizenship is a status from which there can be an exit, whereas womanhood is not, it does not appear to constitute vulnerability to domination.

But there is a compelling reason for thinking that non-citizens are vulnerable to domination as a group: if domination is more than the sum of its parts. Since non-domination requires full incorporation 'into a framework that guards those basic liberties against the control of others' (Pettit 2008, p. 203), mutual knowledge that non-citizens have only partial incorporation might mean they cannot participate in interactions as equals. Without public affirmation and assurance of the denizen's independence from unaccountable power, the status of being a denizen might become a 'badge of vulnerability', to use Pettit's term. On this reading, a 'vulnerability class' is defined not only by the lack of an exit option, but also by the absence of mutual recognition that membership signifies. An examination of how this framework might work in practice will illustrate this point further.

Promoting the non-domination of denizens

Republicans are committed to the reduction of domination wherever possible. But their commitment to non-domination is to a value integral to, if not identical to, citizenship. Thus, Pettit (1997, p. vii) describes his early work as understanding republican freedom 'as equivalent to citizenship in a republic'. From a republican standpoint, enjoyment of non-domination stems from membership in a bounded political community. We therefore need an additional argument to show why migrants' claim to non-domination is made on their host, rather than home, country.

The easiest argument to make here is that the non-domination of denizens is critical to the integrity of republican theory. Non-domination enjoyed by citizens alone is unappealing and self-defeating; it undermines the case made by neo-republicans to be inclusive, non-elitist, and sensitive to contemporary concerns. As Robert Goodin (2003, p. 61) observes, the whole project of reviving republicanism would fail if it were found to rest on a 'status concept'. If the ideal of non-domination as equal status for those of noble birth is replaced by the equal status of citizens, republicanism remains unfit for modern purposes. Goodin presents would-be republicans with the choice of either revising republicanism so that it does not rest on a status concept, or rejecting it altogether. While he advises the latter, the other choice is still open to us: if it can be shown that denizenship is compatible with non-domination, republicanism will have passed the ultimate test.

For those who are unconvinced by this argument, a more compelling argument might be this: non-domination does not mandate the allocation of the same goods to all recipients, just as 'treatment as an equal' does not require 'equal treatment' (Dworkin 1977, p. 227).[9] As such, domination as dependence on unaccountable power allows for substantial variation in the dependence level of migrants, and thus for varying demands on the state. For example, unresponsive democratic institutions are deeply problematic for migrants who have lived in the country for decades or who would otherwise find emigration costly, but are much less troubling for new arrivals with a passport from a liberal democracy. Promoting the non-domination of denizens does not require increasing accountability or empowering denizens up to the level of citizens, or indeed providing them with citizenship from the offset. For the state to track the public good requires taking the interests of denizens into account, but the weight accorded to these interests can be smaller.

That said, there are compelling arguments why denizens ought *not* enjoy non-domination that are worthy of consideration: the contribution objection, the consent objection and the benevolence objection.

The first is a common refrain in many countries grappling with public anxiety about immigration. It states that citizens who have contributed more in taxes and time deserve more in the way of benefits. Since valuing the non-domination of non-citizens alongside that of citizens will not mandate treating non-citizens and citizens equally in all situations, new arrivals are likely to have weaker entitlements. But the problem still stands for groups such as refugees who have contributed little yet have high exit costs of leaving.

One potential response is that we do not generally object when in certain cases the benefits received by citizens outweigh what they have contributed, as Goodin (1988) contends in his comments on obligation and the 'mutual-benefit society'. Goodin's point is that we think the disabled should be entitled to certain goods just by virtue of needing them, not because of what they have contributed. Examples like these are often provided as evidence that our special obligations are grounded in something other than contribution, such as citizenship (Scheffler 2001, Miller 2007). But it might be that dependence better coheres with our intuitions about entitlements to public goods and services than contribution or citizenship. Our strongest intuition about foreigners' use of public services is that people passing through should have no claim on them, but few would argue that permanent residents should have no claim on public resources. In fact, some scholars who believe citizenship grounds special obligations concede that special obligations extend to permanent residents. These theorists might, however, struggle to identify a threshold beyond which someone counts as a permanent resident for the purposes of citizenship obligations. (Two years? Six years?). Since citizenship alone cannot underpin these special rights and duties, we need an alternative criterion. Dependence seems to me as good a principle as any.

The second objection uses the principle of consent to argue that by entering the state, migrants have consented to differential or inferior treatment. Providing them with fewer rights (or, in my terms, not treating them as equivalent to citizens for the purposes of non-domination) is therefore acceptable. In this vein, Daniel Bell (2006) argues that since migrants should be able to choose for themselves whether or not they want to absorb whatever terms offered by a state, insisting on certain rights undermines this choice.[10] In response, most republicans would contend that consent is irrelevant to the moral imperative to reduce domination. For example, Pettit (1996, p. 585) claims we should always aim to reduce domination, whether it 'sprang originally from a contract or not, whether or not it was consensual in origin'.

While I agree with Pettit that consent is irrelevant, even those who believe in the legitimizing potential of consent ought to agree with my conclusions. Consider the notion of a 'dismal choice scenario' (Lovett 2010, p. 148) whereby, generally speaking, people do not enter dominating relationships unless they have no viable alternatives. If a migrant had reasonable alternatives but chose to come to a particular country their dependence would necessarily be low (since they could have gone elsewhere). According to my model they could reasonably be granted fewer rights than citizens or long-term residents – in line with the intuitions of consent theorists. By contrast, a migrant with dismal alternatives would be highly dependent on the option he or she had taken (as it was the only viable option). Surely this scenario would not fulfil the criterion of genuine consent that a consent theorist would demand to justify granting fewer rights. Consent cannot justify tolerating higher levels of domination, but what counts as domination might be more flexible than critics allow, and incorporate some of their intuitions.

The final objection sees domination as a necessary feature in immigrants' transition from denizenship to citizenship, akin to the development of children into adults. In this vein, we might wish to say that the domination of denizens is unproblematic provided it is benevolent, that is, in their interests. Denizens will be much, much better off as a result of being accepted as residents of a liberal state, even if they are not beneficiaries of full non-domination, hence the domination they do experience is of little concern because it is inevitable or in their interests. The logic of the benevolence objection would therefore have us say that state power is problematic only when it is not wielded in the interests of immigrants. Again, Lovett's (2010, pp. 145–147) reading of the benevolence problem for children is illustrative. It is not that the domination itself is good, but that the care relationship provided by the parents is valuable in spite of the domination. Reducing the domination, if at all possible, would be a good thing – it is surely better to protect the rights of children and obligations of parents in law and convention. Similarly, liberal states may – and in many cases do – treat denizens well and promote policies that further the interests of migrants. But if they are not forced to track their interests through various accountability mechanisms, migrants are vulnerable to domination, just as children in a society where children's rights are not protected.

All these three objections are forceful, but ultimately not fatal. In fact, the concept of exit costs emerges as a way to articulate some of the central intuitions of immigration theorists, such as the intuition that new arrivals (all else being equal) might reasonably be allocated fewer of the rights of citizenship. In the final section, I elaborate on the prescriptive implications of my theory.

Denizenship as a status of non-domination?

Like Braithwaite and Pettit, who develop a theory of domination-minimizing criminal justice, I see the potential of non-domination as inspiring an approach for policy-makers rather than prescribing individual policies. Braithwaite and Pettit (1990), p. 86) describe their project as a 'research programme for normative thinking [...] a policy heuristic, though not a policy algorithm'. In a similar vein, I try to outline approaches that policy-makers could adopt to reduce domination, not to dictate precise policies. These recommendations fall into three main groups.

Improving the accountability of countries to their non-citizen population

Accountability, on my account, is a threshold concept, so, in order for non-domination to obtain, three different types of accountability mechanisms need to be accessible: justification, contestation and retribution. Generally, mechanisms for controlling and checking the executive of the sort usually associated with democracies – like judicial review, regular and open elections, a free press, bicameralism, a multi-party system, and so on – increase the first and last of these. The middle one, contestation, requires that accountability is at least to some extent self-initiated or self-controlled. That is, the person subject to the power needs to have some say or sway over how it is wielded; it is not enough that it is subject to external checking mechanisms. This is what republicans have traditionally called 'voice', and it is central to the republican conception of citizenship.

Since migrants who have low exit costs of leaving the state require a lower threshold of accountability, they plausibly do not require this third, middle element of contestation or 'voice'. Migrants in this category include new arrivals who have not yet built up strong emotional and social ties, alongside those who enjoy decent prospects in their home country, citizenship of multiple countries, 'super denizenship' status (citizenship of a European Union member state), considerable financial resources, or internationally desirable skills. In other words, people who could move elsewhere without significant obstacles or considerable loss. Since the coercive power of the state and thus how it both constitutes *imperium* and consolidates *dominium* is less troubling, their accountability threshold can be lower. An alternative way of describing this, following Albert Hirschman (1970), is that the state gains its legitimacy from a different source: from exit, rather than voice. Hirschman's point is that democracy is not the only source of moral legitimacy if membership is voluntary and exit costs are low. The demand for 'voice' increases to the extent that 'exit' is prohibitively costly or infeasible.

Of course, even those with European Union citizenship are likely to become highly dependent after a significant period of time has elapsed, since exit is very costly once people have established social ties. Therefore, after a period of time – perhaps five years or so – all denizens will have reached a level of dependence – requiring the more demanding threshold of accountability to be met.[11] The other precondition for this lower level of accountability is the existence of an alternative agency forcing the host government to track the interests of the denizens in question. Given the limits of human rights courts, the usual way that the requirement of 'contestation' is met is through the denizen's country of origin, such as through adequate diplomatic protection.

National-level diplomatic protection is likely to be most effective in response to drastic rights violations; witness interventions by governments of Western states over the practices at Guantánamo Bay (that had nonetheless variable degrees of success). Even if external protection is effective, an accountability gap may arise from the local interests of migrants. Nothing forces *local* authorities to track the interests of their foreign residents given the absence of diplomatic protection at the local level. Moreover, the democratic mechanisms to consult expatriate citizens on their interests are absent because you generally lose local voting rights if you move out of an area. Since people's interests at the local level are less effectively promoted across borders, granting denizens local voting rights would help mitigate the accountability gap that stems from local interests. Practically speaking, this policy is also a fairly realistic one; many states currently enfranchise their denizen population at a local level.

Highly dependent migrants require a more stringent threshold of accountability to be met. These migrants have no other choice but to remain in their state of residence, thus the coercive power of the state is highly dominating. High dependence is also likely to correlate with ineffectual accountability mechanisms from one's state of origin. A refugee is clearly not going to have their interests tracked by their home government, and governments of countries that produce refugees have less diplomatic influence. By contrast, for those whose high dependence stems from a long period of residence, contestation mechanisms are likely to be ineffective because of the nature of their interests. If a person's interests are largely bound up in their state of origin it is quite straightforward for their government to pursue any interests they have abroad, as these interests probably relate to treatment as a migrant, in other words things subject to diplomatic influence. Once someone's interests are predominantly bound up in their state of residence it becomes harder for their home governments to promote these as they have little sway over issues of domestic policy. This gives us two reasons, then, to support denizen suffrage for highly dependent residents.

On the other hand, enfranchising different groups of migrants after different periods of residence might appear to create a hierarchy of denizens. It would also be very difficult to measure dependence, identify the groups who met the criteria for the higher threshold of accountability, and then administer their voting rights.[12] Granting voting rights to all denizens on the basis that some are highly dependent may therefore be a more appealing policy proposal. While over-inclusive, it is focused on improving the situation of the worst-off in the group. But it means the original principle of dependence is now much changed, as it equates to granting the vote to all denizens regardless of their level of dependence, not because of it. A better option might be to grant denizens voting rights once they are likely to have reached the threshold of dependence, and then supplement the accountability gap with alternative mechanisms to mitigate the domination of those who are highly dependent yet have not lived in the country for long. Even imperfect enfranchisement of denizens *qua* denizens would substantially improve the responsiveness of governments to migrant interests, provided some of the members of each vulnerability group were represented. I think that three to five years would be an appropriate amount of time, but this is difficult to set down in theory.

Empowering migrants against exploitation and abuse

The second group of policies relates to the socioeconomic goods that ought to be available to denizens in order to reduce dominium. Prima facie, a strong case exists for socioeconomic independence. It would prevent migrants from having to stay in exploitative jobs because the alternative is destitution. Social welfare provisions 'shift the relative bargaining power of workers and employers' because they provide people with an alternative so that jobs have to be offered at a market rate (Carens 2008a, p. 432). Similarly, provision of social housing prevents vulnerable migrants from having to rely on charities or favours from informal immigrant networks.

Nevertheless, it might be legitimate to restrict certain migrants' access to some of these benefits, at least for their first few years of residence. What is necessary in this scenario is a certain minimal level of socioeconomic independence rather than the rather fuller package of welfare rights. If a citizen, or highly dependent migrant, found themselves with a choice between a set of exploitative employers they would *have* to take one of these opportunities, whereas someone with low exit costs could move to another country. On the other hand, the sort of means-testing necessary to determine someone's dependence and needs could give the state a large amount of discretion, and as Lovett (2010, p. 198) says 'it will not do to replace the arbitrary charity of private individuals and groups with the arbitrary charity of state welfare agencies'. While erring on the side of caution might require that all migrants be given full socioeconomic rights, in a situation of scarce resources it might be legitimate to restrict access to those who do not have citizenship of a liberal democracy elsewhere.

In any case it is doubtful whether the low exit costs of certain groups of migrants could justify making them pay for access to otherwise universal health care, or restricting access to public education for their children. Even if someone could leave the country at any time, having to pay for medical services or take out health insurance would have a disproportionate impact on poor migrants. Moreover the temptation to gamble and not take out medical insurance might be great, as has been the case in the United States, for less well-off migrants. The kind of unpredictable cost stemming from a serious illness might force them into exploitative relationships in the informal economy.

Citizenship acquisition

Thus far, I have only assessed ways in which to promote non-domination within the status of denizenship. But another way of reducing the domination of denizens is to remove obstacles to becoming a citizen. These two approaches can be balanced against each other; the more resilient the freedom status that denizenship is, the less urgent it is to reduce barriers to citizenship. It follows that the state is entitled to take steps to make citizenship difficult to acquire to the extent that they have improved the status of denizenship. Therefore, the suggestions that I make here are conditional: they depend on what other practices have been adopted. My framework permits states to adopt whichever alternative is compatible with their current policy, cultural goals, and history and tradition. If states wish to make citizenship a hallowed status that is difficult to acquire and thus increase the dependence of denizens on staying in the status of denizenship, they need to ensure that denizenship is not a status of domination.

But this has limitations. Some of the goods of citizenship cannot be disaggregated from its status; except at a very high level of dependence even the small distinctions between citizenship and denizenship are likely to become significant. Some of these goods are legal rights, like the right to travel freely internationally and the right to diplomatic protection abroad. Others are less easily measurable, like the 'intersubjective' benefit of knowing you are in possession of a 'comparable social standing with the other' (Pettit 1997, p. 87). The former are not necessary conditions of non-domination, as they do not pertain to the institutions of the state. But simply having fewer rights than citizens, even if not strictly the sort of rights required for non-domination, consolidates the hierarchy between citizens and non-citizens. I am therefore sceptical that without formal citizenship the full extent of non-domination will be possible. Even if many of the goods of citizenship, including socioeconomic rights and political participation, have been disaggregated from its role as a formal status, the intersubjective benefits that come with being a full member of a community are more difficult to extend. Moreover, they are unlikely to be the sort of things that can be legislated for, as they pertain to citizens' mutual recognition of their shared membership.

We should therefore reduce dependence on the status of denizenship (the costs of exit) by decreasing obstacles to acquiring citizenship. Barriers to citizenship should be parsimonious, non-arbitrary and should not impose disproportionate burdens on certain groups. A further suggestion would be to minimize the discretionary power of officials, that is, the power to make subjective judgements rather than being bound by external rules. In terms of commonly raised issues about citizenship tests, language stipulations, and so on, my account indicates that it would be better for the government to provide the means for denizens to get to a desired level of language attainment rather than impose a condition that they demonstrate such a level. These conditions increase the dependence of denizens on citizenship, but are likely to fall disproportionately on the uneducated or badly off (because they have to work longer hours to make ends meet) who have higher exit costs of leaving the state. The combination of dependence on denizenship, and dependence on remaining in the state, increases the level of domination these groups are subject to.[15] Finally, my framework would rule out imposing large costs on acquiring citizenship, and would advocate providing disadvantaged migrants with the opportunity to stagger their payments (and indeed any immigration-related payments) in order to reduce dependence.

Conclusion

This paper has sought to demonstrate the potential of domination to inform moral thinking about denizens to both republican and immigration theorists. I have outlined a conceptual framework for identifying the conditions under which denizenship is problematic, and in particular, dominating, and demonstrated what this might recommend in policy terms. I hope to have shown that domination can make sense of some well-established intuitions in immigration theory, while offering new material for thinking through some of the more thorny issues on the political agenda.

Acknowledgements

An earlier version of the paper was presented at 'Non-Citizens in Liberal Democracies – Republican and Liberal Perspectives' conference held at the University of Wales, Newport, in March 2011. Thanks are owed to all the participants, including Iseult Honohan, Marit Hovdal Moan, David Owen and Stuart White. My thinking was also shaped by conversations with Gideon Calder, Sarah Fine, Jonathan Seglow and Albert Weale. I am grateful for insightful comments from an anonymous reviewer. I owe a debt of gratitude to my PhD supervisors, Cécile Laborde and Richard Bellamy.

Funding

This paper forms one output from PhD research funded by the UK Arts and Humanities Research Council.

Notes

1. This association between republicanism and the bounded state is beginning to change as part of a broader project of reinventing republicanism for modern conditions of globalization, mass migration and pluralism. For example, Cécile Laborde (2010) has developed a republican theory of global justice. In this volume, Iseult Honohan and Sarah Fine consider how republicans might address dominating migration controls.
2. Other normative theorists have examined the status and entitlements of particular groups, such as refugees, unauthorized migrants, or seasonal workers (Bosniak 2007, Carens 2008a, 2008b). This paper examines commonalities between these types of non-citizen status in order to make sense of the status of denizenship in general; hence, I will not discuss these theorists directly here.
3. Pettit has used different terminology subsequently, such as 'alien control' (Pettit 2008, p. 103). In my view, the formulation in *Republicanism* (1997) is the clearest, so I stick with it here.

4. They are also, crucially, subject to these features of power in a way that tourists or visitors are not. Although it is beyond the remit of this paper to consider in detail the relevant differences between denizens and tourists, this is clearly central to our understanding of denizenship. I suspect – and hope – that my principle of exit costs will allow us to codify effectively the relevant differences in a way that is compatible with our fundamental intuitions about the entitlements of denizens vis-à-vis tourists.
5. The highly skilled, for example, will be in demand and thus literally able to 'take their business elsewhere'.
6. Joseph Carens (2010) suggests that these themselves ground moral entitlements; hence, length of residence is correlated with the strength of moral claims made by resident non-citizens on their state of residence.
7. In Lovett's (2010, pp. 52–54) discussion of dependence on employers, he contends that dependence on one employer need not come only from inability to leave, but from lack of other better options. Thus, the existence of numerous opportunities for employment in exploitative work does not, in itself, reduce the dependence on one exploitative employer.
8. While some would argue that these visas are inherently wrong, I think that it is at least plausible that in some limited circumstances they might be tolerable, namely for a very short period.
9. Pettit (1997, p. 111) also makes the connection between the 'egalitarian commitment' of non-domination and Dworkin's principle that people should be treated as equals.
10. Will Kymlicka (1995, p. 96) has put forward a similar argument against equal cultural rights: immigrants occupy a different status to cultural minorities, as unlike the latter by choosing to immigrate they 'voluntarily relinquish some of the rights that go along with their original national membership'.
11. As Carens (2002) notes, it is nigh impossible for philosophers to determine the precise threshold for claims to citizenship or its benefits.
12. Of course, this problem does not just arise for my model of democracy. Whatever principle underpins the case for democracy there is always a degree of generalization in deciding who is eligible. For example, the argument that excluding children is justifiable because they do not yet have fully developed capacities can be countered by the point that some children are responsible, knowledgeable, and capable enough to vote in their teens, while some adults never attain the desirable qualities (Weale 2007). Deciding who is eligible is therefore always going to involve some degree of shorthand.
13. Note that on this account it is the fact that such barriers would leave many groups effectively dominated, rather than the content of the proposals as such, that make obstacles good or bad. While this implies that language tests are no less problematic than citizenship tests, promoting the development of these capacities is more desirable to making them preconditions of acquiring citizenship.

Notes on contributor

Meghan Benton is a Policy Analyst at the Migration Policy Institute, a think tank based in Washington, DC. Previously, she was a researcher at University College London where she completed her PhD on republicanism and denizenship. She has written on a range of immigration and integration questions, including on exploitation, immigrants' occupational mobility and multiculturalism. She is also currently working on the question of how immigration theorists and immigration policy-makers might better learn from one another.

References

Bauböck, R., 1994. Changing the boundaries of citizenship: the inclusion of immigrants in democratic polities. *In*: R. Bauböck, ed. *From aliens to citizens: redefining the status of immigrants in Europe*. Avebury: Aldershot, UK.

Bauböck, R., 2009. The rights and duties of external citizenship. *Citizenship studies*, 13 (5), 475–499.

Bell, D., 2006. Justice for migrant workers? the case of migrant domestic workers in East Asia. *Beyond liberal democracy: political thinking in an east asian context*. Princeton, NJ: Princeton University Press, 281–322.

Bellamy, R., 2007. *Political constitutionalism: a republican defence of the constitutionality of democracy*. Cambridge: Cambridge University Press.

Benton, M., 2010. The Tyranny of the Enfranchised Majority? the Accountability of States to their Non-Citizen Population. *Res publica*, 16 (4), 397–413.

Bohman, J., 2007. *Democracy across borders: from dêmos to dêmoi*. Cambridge: MIT Press.

Bosniak, L., 2007. The undocumented immigrant: contending policy approaches. *In*: C.M. Swain, ed. *Debating immigration*. Cambridge: Cambridge University Press.

Braithwaite, J. and Pettit, P., 1990. *Not just deserts: a republican theory of criminal justice*. Oxford: Clarendon.

Carens, J., 2002. Citizenship and civil society: what rights for residents? *In*: R. Hansen and P. Weil, eds. *Dual nationality, social rights, and federal citizenship in the US and Europe: the reinvention of citizenship*. New York and Oxford: Berghahn Books.

Carens, J., 2008a. Live-in Domestics, Seasonal Workers, and Others Hard to Locate on the Map of Democracy. *Journal of political philosophy*, 16 (4), 419–445.

Carens, J., 2008b. The Rights of Irregular Migrants. *Ethics & international affairs*, 22 (2), 163–186.

Carens, J., 2010. *Immigrants and the right to stay*. Cambridge, M.A.: MIT Press.

Carter, I., 2008. How are power and unfreedom related? *In*: C. Laborde and J. Maynor, eds. *Republicanism and political theory*. Oxford: Blackwell.

Dworkin, R., 1977. *Taking rights seriously*. Cambridge, M.A.: Harvard University Press.

Fine, S., 2014. Non-Domination and Immigration Control. *Critical review of international social and political philosophy*, 10–30.

Goodin, R.E., 1988. What is so special about our fellow countrymen? *Ethics*, 98 (4), 663–686.

Goodin, R.E., 2003. Folie républicaine. *Annual review of political science*, 6, 55–76.

Hampshire, J., 2009. Becoming citizens: naturalization in the liberal state. *In*: G. Calder, P. Cole and J. Seglow, eds. *Citizenship acquisition and national belonging: Migration, membership and the liberal democratic state*. Palgrave Macmillan: Basingstoke.

Hirschman, A.O., 1970. *Exit, voice, and loyalty*. Cambridge: Cambridge University Press.

Honohan, I., 2014. Domination and Migration: An Alternative Approach to the Legitimacy of Migration Controls. *Critical review of international social and political philosophy*, 31–48.

Kymlicka, W., 1995. *Multicultural citizenship: a liberal theory of minority rights*. Oxford: Clarendon Press.

Laborde, C., 2010. Republicanism and Global Justice: A Sketch. *European journal of political theory*, 9 (1), 48–69.

Laborde, C. and Maynor, J., 2008. The republican contribution. *In*: C. Laborde and J. Maynor, eds. *Republicanism and political theory*. Oxford: Blackwell.

Lovett, F., 2006. Republicanism [online]. The Stanford Encyclopaedia of Philosophy. Available from: http://plato.stanford.edu/entries/republicanism [Accessed 28 August 2013].

Lovett, F., 2010. *A general theory of domination and justice*. Oxford: Oxford University Press.

Miller, D., 2007. *National responsibility and global justice*. Oxford: Oxford University Press.

Pettit, P., 1996. Freedom as antipower. *Ethics*, 106 (3), 576–604.

Pettit, P., 1997. *Republicanism: a theory of freedom and government*. Oxford: Oxford University Press.

Pettit, P., 2008. The Basic Liberties. *In*: M.H. Kramer, C. Grant, B. Colburn and A. Hatzistavrou, eds. *The Legacy of H.L.A. Hart: Legal, political, and moral philosophy*. Oxford: Oxford University Press.

Scheffler, S., 2001. *Boundaries and allegiances: problems of justice and responsibility in liberal thought*. Oxford: Oxford University Press.

Seglow, J., 2009. Arguments for naturalisation. *Political studies*, 57 (4), 788–804.

Shapiro, I. and Hacker-Cordón, C., 1999. Outer edges and inner edges. *In*: I. Shapiro and C. Hacker-Cordón, eds. *Democracy's edges*. Cambridge: Cambridge University Press.

Skinner, Q., 1997. *Liberty before liberalism*. Cambridge: Cambridge University Press.

Skinner, Q., 2008. Freedom as the absence of arbitrary power. *In*: C. Laborde and J. Maynor, eds. *Republicanism and political theory*. Oxford: Blackwell.

Walzer, M., 1983. *Spheres of justice: a defence of pluralism and equality*. Oxford: Robertson.

Weale, A., 2007. *Democracy*. Basingstoke: Palgrave Macmillan.

Unequal residence statuses and the ideal of non-domination

Marit Hovdal-Moan

Philosophy, Norwegian University of Science and Technology (NTNU), Trondheim, Norway

I propose a principle of non-domination as a benchmark for assessing the justifiability of unequal residence statuses for non-nationals in liberal democracies. This has advantages over the principles of equality and rights alike, in accommodating both the inclusive and exclusive logics of liberal democratic citizenship. Non-domination requires the state to grant upon first admission a degree of inclusion in the social privileges of citizenship that is sufficient to guard against the most severe forms of domination in social relationships. However, as resident non-nationals become more permanent and come to be in relationships open to other, if less severe forms of domination, it requires gradually increasing the degree of inclusion, over time, to protect non-nationals against these forms of domination also, and, finally, eventually giving them access to the sites of political decision-making that contribute to shaping the background conditions for independent action in social relationships.

Introduction

My aim in this paper is to propose a principle for assessing the justice of forms of unequal residence statuses for non-nationals in liberal democracies. An unequal residence status is a formal status that grants its holder only a certain *degree* of inclusion in the rights of citizenship, and hence also subjects her or him to a degree of exclusion from full citizenship, both with respect to the degree of participation in political and economic activities that it offers, and the range of public goods and services to which it gives access. Liberal democratic states operate with several models of unequal resident statuses for non-nationals, all of which 'differentiate the political, social, and civil rights of [non-nationals] from those of citizens' (Galloway 2008, p. 37; see also Soysal 1994, Cholewinski 2004, Santoro *et al.* 2004, Howard 2009). Resident non-nationals who are subject to these and other forms of rights restrictions are what Elisabeth Cohen has termed 'semi-citizens' (Cohen 2009), and include temporary migrant workers, foreign students, permanent residents in a

Schengen country holding a European Union passport, post-colonial subjects, asylum-seekers and irregular immigrants.[1] These groups all are accorded a residence status that is differentiated from that of citizens. However, status-wise they differ widely with respect to the packages of citizenship rights and responsibilities that they enjoy, depending on the model, or form, of residence status that they hold.

Theorists concerned with the question of state duties towards resident non-nationals seem generally to agree that a practice of partial inclusion of resident non-nationals into the rights and responsibilities of citizenship is morally permissible, provided that they are given the opportunity to naturalize after a period of time (Bauböck 1994, Fiss 1999, Carens 2002, 2008a, 2008b, Benhabib 2004, Bosniak 2006, Sangiovanni 2007). However, they offer different accounts of how this position can be justified, and consequently different accounts of which packages of rights resident non-nationals should be accorded at the different stages towards full inclusion.[2] In this paper I seek to explain how this consensus position regarding the moral permissibility of the practice of unequal residence statuses for non-nationals could be justified, basing the argument on an ideal of non-domination.

Following Frank Lovett (2010), I understand non-domination as independence from social relationships in which some other person has unconstrained power to change what you would otherwise prefer to do. I argue that this is preferable in this context to current alternative ideals, notably those of equality of legal and democratic standing, and individual rights. The three ideals all follow from the concept of liberal democratic citizenship, which I take to reflect liberal democratic states' *own understanding* of morally justifiable relations between the state and individuals who are subject to the state's jurisdiction, and between residents in that state. I argue that when considering the practical implications of meeting these ideals, only that of non-domination can accommodate both the inclusive and the exclusive logics of membership contained in the concept of liberal-democratic citizenship.

The importance of paying heed to both these logics follows from a proviso central to the argument in this paper, namely that if moral judgment is to move actual practice, it must accommodate not only the imperatives of moral universalist principles, but also the prudential and institutional constraints on the practical feasibility of a given principle. One such constraint in this context is the moral motivation of a liberal democratic citizenry, which I take to value citizenship, as a marker not only of inclusion, but also of community, belonging and identity. Any principle meant to guide state policies towards resident non-nationals that entailed discarding one of these values would therefore be unfeasible because unable to motivate citizens and move actual practice.

In reflecting on which principle can best accommodate both values I apply a contextualist method – one which looks to existing practice to gain insight into how best to bring relevant but conflicting normative values into a 'reflective equilibrium'[3] at a conceptual level. The relevant practice in this case is that of liberal democracies' partial inclusion of resident non-nationals, and the possibility for some categories of resident non-nationals to gain an increasing number of citizenship rights, and eventually citizenship, as time passes.[4] The idea contained in this practice of a step-by-step inclusion in, and hence a decreasing degree of exclusion from, citizenship over time seems prima facie reasonable, *provided that* we want to pay heed to both the exclusivist and inclusivist aspects of the ideal of liberal democratic citizenship. This is not uncritically to adopt the status quo as a standard for moral reflection. Rather, it is based on the assumption that practice can contain moral wisdom that has yet to be adopted and conceptualized at the level of theory, to paraphrase Joseph Carens (Carens 2000).[5] However, as Carens also acknowledges, the insight of practice needs to be checked against 'the critical perspective of theory' (Carens 2000, p. 4). To retain a critical distance from practice, therefore, I move back and forth between theory and practice to ensure that values, principles and practice inform each other.

In what follows, I elaborate on the contrasting normative logics integral to the concept of liberal democratic citizenship, and argue that, with respect to resident non-nationals, the practical realization of the ideal of equality and individual rights would entail discarding one of these logics. In the last part of the paper I seek to show that, by contrast, the practical realization of the ideal of non-domination would pay heed to both. Specifically, it would yield a model of differentiated residence statuses, which would, on the one hand, require no more than a *partial* inclusion in the privileges of citizenship upon first admission to residency, but then require that the degree of inclusion for resident non-nationals increase gradually, over time. This model would also fit the idea reflected in existing practice of a step-by-step inclusion in citizenship over time. It moves beyond actual practice, however, in requiring that the state apply this model to all resident non-nationals, rather than only to some categories, as the practice is today. Moreover, a principle of non-domination would also serve as a moral yardstick for judging whether the specific forms and degrees that partial inclusion could take, and the form that it currently takes in actual practice, qualify as just at each step towards full inclusion.

Differentiated residence statuses and the normative orientations of citizenship

Following Cohen, I define resident non-nationals, with reference not to some social identity, but to their position within a political structure, and the rights that they can claim within it. Resident non-nationals represent a vast array of what Cohen would call 'administratively distinct semi-citizenships' (Cohen 2009, p. 147). These range from the undocumented migrant, whose rights are cut to a bare minimum and who are constantly subject to the threat of deportation, to the permanent resident with membership of a transnational organisation such as the European Union, whose rights are almost indistinguishable from those of the full citizen. Non-national semi-citizens who occupy points in between these poles include asylum-seekers, refugees, seasonal and other low-skilled temporary migrant workers, high-skilled workers, and migrants who have been granted a right to enter the country on the basis of family reunion.[6] Each administrative form that semi-citizenship may take in the case of non-nationals comes with different packages of rights and responsibilities for the individual. This means that, depending on the package of rights that they are accorded, non-national semi-citizens stand in widely different structural positions vis-à-vis the state, citizens and other semi-citizens. The way in which semi-citizenship structurally shapes the life of non-nationals in disadvantageous ways will therefore also vary.

Judging by the internal normative logics of the concept of liberal democratic citizenship it is not immediately clear what to make of liberal democracies' practice of differentiated residence statuses for non-nationals, normatively speaking. The moral universalist 'oughts' of citizenship suggests that nothing short of full inclusion of non-nationals upon first admission to residency is morally permissible, including equal legal standing before the law, equal access to civil, political and social rights, and equal access to participate in political decision-making procedures. However, by contrast, citizenship's ethico-political 'ought' suggests that the community is justified in treating resident non-citizens differentially, in order to further a particular conception of the good society, and to safeguard the community's perceived long-term interests. Let me briefly elaborate.

The ideal of equal and inclusive citizenship is reflected in the main conceptions of citizenship in contemporary citizenship theory: according to the conception of citizenship as a *formal legal standing*, citizenship stands for everyone's equal legal standing before the law. On the understanding of citizenship as entitlement and *enjoyment of rights*, it stands for everyone's equal entitlement to and enjoyment of civil, political and social rights. The conception of citizenship as *political participation* sees it as a matter of equal participation of everyone in political decision-making procedures (Barbalet, 1988, Gunsteren 1998, Heater 1999, Bellamy and Palumbo 2010). Even the 'politics of recognition' discourse is conducted in the language of citizenship, with an insistence on the importance of recognizing difference to achieve true inclusion and equality (Young 1990, Benhabib 1996). On this reading, legal differentiations of resident non-nationals, and their consequent status inferiority, represent a major moral embarrassment for liberal democracies as they contradict the standards of universal inclusion and equality that the ideal of liberal democratic citizenship embodies (see also Cole 2000).

And yet, the concept of liberal democratic citizenship does not provide an unambiguous standard for judging the justifiability of subjecting resident non-nationals to unequal residence statuses. Indeed, it is possible in theory to reject the above conclusion on the basis of a second normative orientation integral to the ideal of citizenship itself, namely that of demarcating and maintaining the boundaries of a particular political community. The inclusive dimension of citizenship assumes a bounded political community and a fixed population of members of that community. Citizenship's orientation towards equality and inclusion applies to this fixed population of members. Indeed, citizenship is a status that demarcates who belongs and who do not belong as full members of a particular bounded community. But this means that the concept of citizenship also assumes a population of non-members, which consequently falls outside the scope of the inclusive principles that it embodies. As such it serves to mark the political community's threshold, just as the borderlines on a map marking out the political community's territory. This is the exclusive dimension of citizenship, which constrains the scope of its inclusive orientation (Brubaker 1992, Bauböck 1994, Miller 2000, Benhabib 2004, Bosniak 2006).[7]

Due to its contrasting normative logics, the ideal-typical model of liberal democratic citizenship seems both to prohibit and permit differentiated residence statuses for resident non-nationals. Which normative logic should then apply when assessing the justifiability of the practice of differentiation in liberal democracies, given an understanding of the concept of citizenship as an ideal model of just relations between the state and individuals subject to its jurisdiction? Presuming that not only internal conceptual coherence, but also practical feasibility is a necessary criterion when analysing the normative meaning of concepts, I want to suggest that neither of the logics can be entirely disposed of when assessing the justifiability of differentiated residence statuses for non-citizens in liberal democracies, lest we fracture the very idea of citizenship as both liberal *and* democratic. We need to pay heed to both.

The concept of liberal democratic citizenship rests upon certain core values, which give it normative meaning, and which also explain its contrasting normative orientations. Core among these values are equal legal and democratic standing, and individual rights, which can be traced to the early Athenian and Roman understandings of citizenship, respectively (Pocock 1995), but also the value of freedom, which can be linked to the reason why citizens should enjoy equal democratic standing and equal access to political, economic and social rights in the first place: citizens should treat each other as free individuals able of agency, securing each other's freedom from arbitrary interference by the state as well as by their co-citizens (Bobbio 1990, Bellamy and Palumbo 2010). Depending on which of these values one stresses, the normative meaning of liberal democratic citizenship becomes more or less inclusive/exclusive. In the following section I discuss which of these three core values can best accommodate *both* of its contrastive normative orientations: that of equality, individual rights, or freedom. I argue that only the latter, understood in terms of non-domination, can.

Differentiated residence statuses, equality and individual rights

Given the central place of the value of equality in the universalist ideal of citizenship, a principle of equality seems a reasonable starting point for reflection on the justifiability of forms of differentiated residence statuses for non-nationals in liberal democracies. I want to argue, however, that the concept of equality is unhelpful in thinking about the question of justifiable differentiated statuses.

There are procedural and substantive interpretations of the principle of equality. On the former reading, it entails only that everyone counts from a moral point of view, and that the state's treatment of them is therefore morally relevant. The recognition that someone counts from a moral viewpoint does not tell us how that someone is to be treated; only that 'there are moral considerations that directly govern and limit our treatment of that thing' (Kagan 1998, p. 171, also Benn 1967). In other words, what the principle of equal moral consideration does in the first instance is rule out certain forms of treatment of persons, such as, for instance, forms of conduct whose effect on others benefit us to the detriment of their interests or needs. It also rules out treating people differently without giving reasons for doing so, or giving reasons that are based on prejudice or other forms of arbitrary reasons, like for instance that of denying non-nationals access to basic healthcare because they are dark-skinned.

However, interpreted in this weak sense, the principle of equality does not say whether non-nationals have a claim to receiving any particular social goods from the state, or in what proportion they ought to receive them, be they rights, or resources, or whatever it is that is being distributed. On a procedural reading, then, the principle of equality is in theory compatible with a society in which non-nationals are entirely excluded from society's systems of social protection as well as its political decision-making processes. But this conclusion leaves no room for the inclusive aspect of the ideal-typical model of citizenship.

A substantive interpretation of the principle of equality creates the opposite problem, namely that it leaves no room for the exclusive dimension of citizenship, and so no room for defending the state's right to regulate the composition of the population to whom state obligations are owed. To illustrate this point, consider the effect of applying a substantive interpretation of the principle of equality to the sphere of political participation. Treating non-nationals on a par with citizens in this sphere will require that they be included in all political decision-making processes on same terms as citizens. However, that would not be compatible with the claim that political communities have a right to self-determination in matters to do with non-nationals' entering the territory and access to membership. If one accepts that political communities enjoy this right, one cannot in the next breath argue that political communities are unjustified in excluding non-nationals from political processes of deliberation on the basis that they are affected by its results. As Seyla Benhabib and others have pointed out (Benhabib 2004, p. 15; see also Whelan, 1983):

> a shared feature of all norms of membership is that those who are affected by the consequences of these norms and, in the first place, by criteria of exclusion, *per definitionem*, cannot be party to their articulation. Membership norms affect those who are not members precisely by distinguishing insiders from outsiders, citizens from non-citizens.

If those affected by the norms of membership and exclusion were included in the process of determining what those norms should be, they would no longer be excluded, which would remove the need for determining norms of membership in the first place. A principle of substantive equally would collapse the distinction between citizens and non-nationals, and so leave no room for the exclusive dimension of the ideal-typical model of citizenship.

One way of circumventing the problem to which a substantive principle of equality gives rise, is to look to the ideal of individual rights to ground claims about state obligations towards resident non-nationals (e.g. Miller 2008). This makes sense, since we are concerned with the state's obligations towards individuals rather than towards citizens. A rights-based principle also fits with the widely shared understanding of citizenship as entitlement to civil, political, and social rights.

However, in this context individual rights must necessarily refer to some version of *human* rights; that is, rights that are grounded on the universal moral value of personhood rather than membership in a political community. Given the proviso that our principle must pay heed to both logics of citizenship, this strategy is problematic. First, because it allows a narrow, negative interpretation of the rights to which resident non-nationals are entitled; that is, liberty rights. Liberty rights are commonly thought of as rights not to be interfered with (Cranston 1973, Jones 1994; more generally, see Shue 1996). On this understanding of human rights, the state owes resident non-nationals little more than respect for the procedural and material restrictions on state power that can be said to follow from negative rights (e.g. refraining from arresting or detaining anyone save when lawful and after conviction by a competent court; and refraining from subjecting anyone to degrading or inhumane treatment). It seems to follow from a negative interpretation of human rights, then, that as long as the state respects these minimum duties, it is justified in excluding resident non-nationals from all other privileges of citizenship. But this conclusion seems unsatisfactory from the viewpoint of citizenship's inclusive orientation.

To circumvent this problem one could argue either that the state has certain positive obligations to provide non-nationals with socioeconomic goods and services, which follow from the state's negative duties, or that socioeconomic human rights exist independent of the state's negative duties. However, with respect to the first approach, even on a generous interpretation, there is a limit to the range of positive rights one can plausibly derive from the right to non-interference. For instance, it seems difficult to justify a right to political participation on any level of governance on this basis. And an indefinite exclusion of resident non-nationals from participating in political activity is incompatible with the internal logic of democratic citizenship (on this last point, see Walzer 1983, ch. 2).

Regarding the second approach, once we add socioeconomic rights to the list of resident non-nationals' human rights, we run into a problem of indeterminacy. Depending on how we define human well-being, the list of welfare rights can be made so long that the distinction between citizens and non-nationals status collapses. The same problem appears if we use the socioeconomic rights to which citizens have access as a measure for which human rights resident non-nationals should enjoy (see, for example, Carens' approach in Carens 2008a), rather than some objective definition of human well-being: if our starting point is the rights that citizens enjoy, there is no non-arbitrary way of drawing the line between the socioeconomic goods and services to which resident non-citizens should have access and the goods and services that should be reserved for citizens, or between socioeconomic rights and, say, political and cultural rights. Again, the list of rights to which resident non-nationals would be entitled would collapse the distinction between non-nationals and citizens and so is unsatisfactory from the perspective of citizenship's exclusivist commitment.[8]

It seems that, in practice, the principles of equality and rights can accommodate only one of the following two models of statuses for resident non-nationals: on the first model, they would be subject to full or nearly full exclusion from society's political decision-making procedures and systems of social protection, indefinitely; on the other model, access to residency would involve full inclusion in society's political decision-making procedures and systems of social protection from day one, thereby collapsing the distinction between citizens and non-nationals. Neither of these principles, therefore, seems able in practice to accommodate both the inclusive and exclusive commitments of the concept of liberal democratic citizenship.

Differentiated residence statuses and the ideal of non-domination

As an alternative to the above approaches, I want to suggest that, in the case of resident non-nationals, the practical realization of a principle based on the value of freedom understood as non-domination would accommodate both the inclusive and exclusive normative orientations of citizenship. Moreover, it would yield a model of residence statuses for resident non-nationals that resonates with the idea of a step-by-step inclusion into citizenship; an idea which is reflected in actual practice, and which appears prima facie reasonable, provided that we want to accommodate both of the normative orientations of liberal democratic citizenship. A principle of non-domination is therefore better suited than a principle of equality or individual rights to assess the moral justifiability of models of unequal residence statuses for non-nationals. It is substantial enough to avoid the problem of procedural equality, yet not so substantial as to require equal treatment of non-nationals from the first day of residence. It would require an increase in resident non-nationals' entitlements over time, but it does not require for its fulfilment that they enjoy equal amounts of some benefit or right for a residence status to qualify as just. A principle of non-domination demands more than would follow from a negative theory of human rights. However, it is self-limiting, and so avoids the problem of indeterminacy to which a theory of human rights based on some notion of human well-being gives rise. Let me elaborate.

Following Frank Lovett, I understand non-domination to refer to a condition under which you are independent from social relationships in which some other person has more social power than you, and can use this power unconstrained by external checks to change what you would otherwise prefer to do (Lovett 2010).[9] Put differently, you enjoy non-domination when, in a social relationship, you can decide which purpose or end to pursue, independent of someone else's subjective, or unchecked, will. You *depend* on a social relationship if you are unable to exit it without what you consider to be a too high cost. That others have social power over you means that they are able to change what you would otherwise prefer to do, or prevent you from doing what you would otherwise do. However, this imbalance in social power only becomes an element of domination to the extent that it can be used *without constraint by external factors*, such as effective rules, rights, and procedures that are common knowledge to all parties involved.

Turning the picture around, we see that the following three conditions must obtain to say that a person does not enjoy non-domination, but instead is *dominated*: (1) she must be in a social relationship on which she depends to some degree, in the sense that she considers the cost of exit to be very high or too high to bear; (2) there must be an imbalance of social power between her and the person with whom she is in the social relationship, and (3) the other person must be able to use his or her social power arbitrarily, that is unconstrained by external rules (Lovett 2010, p. 120). As a main rule, if these three conditions do *not jointly* obtain, the person cannot be said to suffer domination. Moreover, the person with less social power can decide to *trade away* legal protections against the arbitrary power of the other person, in order to achieve or safeguard what she perceives as a basic need. Even if the person with the greater social power is externally constrained, domination will obtain as long as the person with less social power lacks the means to secure the basic need that she achieves through the social relationship (Lovett 2010, pp. 190–195).

So for instance, a tenant is in a social relationship with his landlord, on which he depends to a lesser or greater degree because he considers the exit costs too high (say, because the rent for other one and two-bedroom apartments has increased so much that he cannot afford it). Because the landlord can decide to end the contract, there is also an imbalance in the social power between the two. However, as long as the landlord's social power is constrained by effectively implemented legal rules and regulations known to both parties, such as restrictions on the termination of contracts and legal sanctions should the landlord seek to take advantage of the tenant's dependency, the relationship cannot be said to constitute one of domination. Yet, if the tenant has no access to publicly funded entitlements that may help him secure an alternative shelter, and he decides for that reason to trade away contractual protections against the arbitrary power of the landlord in order to keep the apartment, the relationship turns into one of domination.

The above example serves to illustrate an important aspect of the meaning of domination, and hence non-domination, as the concept is used here. Namely that, should a person in a social relationship use his greater social power to change what the other person would otherwise prefer to do (e.g. terminate the contract), the interference does not constitute domination as long as the use of that power is in accordance with commonly known rules, rights, and procedures, and as long as the person with less social power is protected from trading away these external protections, by, for instance, publicly funded entitlements.

However, a person can also be dominated without any actual interference taking place, and without there being a high probability that actual interference will take place (Skinner 1998). So for instance, imagine a society in which there are no external constraints on a landlords' power to end a contract in the form on commonly known rules and regulations. The fact that the landlord never uses his greater social power to end the rental contract at his will, and that the probability that he will ever do so is very low, does not mean that the tenant therefore does not suffer domination. In the absence of external constraints on the landlords greater social power, the tenant remains dependent on the landlord's will in the sense that, if the landlord wanted to, he could decide to end the contract as he pleases, and the tenant would be in no position to challenge that decision. In other words, the degree of *probable* interference is unimportant to the question of whether domination obtains.[10] After all, dominated parties can learn to predict the dominating parties' moods and preferences and act in a way that reduces the probability of interference to a minimum (Pettit 1997, pp. 86–88, Skinner 1998, Costa 2009). The entire pattern of conduct of the less powerful person in a social relationship will thus reflect the subjective will of the more powerful person, even in the absence of interference.

The paragraph above illustrates a second important aspect of domination as it is understood here, namely that it is not a specific outcome or pattern of results of a social relationship that determines whether domination obtains, but its *structure*. That is, it is not the extent of arbitrary interference in a social relationship, or who on the whole can be said to benefit from the relationship, that determine whether or not it is one of domination. Rather, it is the opportunities for independent action available to the parties in the relationship that decide whether it constitutes one of domination (Lovett 2010, pp. 40–47). These are determined, not only by the individual endowment of the parties to that relationship or their unilateral decisions, but by the structural environment in which that relationship is embedded and the options for action that this environment enables. The structural environment refers here to what Rawls terms 'society's basic structure'; that is, the relatively stable political and social institutions and practices that 'distribute fundamental rights and duties and determine the division of advantages from social cooperation', and which provide ground for different expectations of life depending on the social position one holds within that structure (Rawls 1971, pp. 6–10). A society's background conditions include the rules and regulations that restrict state power, regulate market exchanges and labour market relations, and the principal social arrangements, such as the system of publicly funded entitlements. Included are also major social institutions such as the system of private property and the (monogamous) family. These background conditions attach opportunities and disadvantages to social positions, which in turn affect the room that each party to a social relationship has for independent action (Young 2007, pp. 168, 169).

I will argue that the principle of non-domination, based on the definition outlined above, is particularly well suited for constructing a principle that can serve as a normative benchmark for justifiable models of residence statuses for non-nationals in liberal democracies. There are two reasons for this. First, that it requires for its fulfilment an only partial inclusion of non-nationals into the social privileges of citizenship upon their taking residence in the state, to guard against the most severe forms of domination that can arise in the context of social relationships. Second, that it nonetheless requires a gradual increase of rights over time to protect against additional, albeit less severe, forms of domination in social relationships that emerge over time, and eventually also to provide access to the sites of political decision-making that contribute to form the background conditions for independent action in social relationships.

One reason that our principle of non-domination requires only partial inclusion into the privileges of citizenship for new residents is its understanding of domination as occurring primarily in the context of social relationships. A social relationship is one in which the persons engaged in social interaction takes into account the likely actions of the other(s) before deciding what to do. By contrast, we often engage in social interaction with others without taking account of their likely actions before deciding what to do; that is, without acting strategically in relation to them. This is the case in all interaction with others where the 'aggregate outcome of their actions are highly predictable and unaffected by my own decisions' such as for instance exchanges between buyer and seller in a competitive market (Lovett 2010, pp. 35, 36). This linkage between domination and strategic social interaction means that domination as defined here can only occur in what one may think of as *direct* social relationships, where a person's decision how to act depends on the likely purposeful actions of one or more *particular* agent (as opposed to indirect social relationships, say between a resident non-national and everyone contributing to upholding an immigration system that excludes resident non-nationals from the vote). On this understanding, domination follows most readily where there are (1) few or no external constraints on the exercise of imbalances of social power in social relationships, or (2) little or no access to publicly funded entitlements that protect people against the choice to trade away the protection against arbitrary uses of social power provided by formal rules and regulations.

This emphasis on direct social relationships as the primary locus of domination entails that *civil* and *social* disabilities (e.g. bars on employment, exclusion from public schools, healthcare, food stamps, public shelter) rather than *political* ones (exclusion from the vote), to borrow Fiss's (1999) terms, constitute a principal and immediate source of domination, as the former has the most direct impact on persons' vulnerability to become subject to some particular other's subjective will. It follows that the equal right to participate in democratic decision-making procedures is not in itself a necessary condition to fulfil the principle of non-domination as defined here. This is a second reason why our principle of non-domination requires only partial inclusion into the privileges of citizenship for new residents. Admittedly, it seems intuitively odd to deny that excluding a group of residents from the vote at all levels of political decision-making constitutes a form of domination. However, given the understanding of arbitrary use of social power that informs our definition of domination, according to which the use of social power is arbitrary only to the extent that it is not externally and effectively constrained by laws and regulations known to all parties, institutionalized discrimination does not necessarily amount to domination, even if it can be deemed wrong for other reasons (Lovett 2010, pp. 117–119). As long as the law excluding resident non-nationals from the vote is known to all parties, so that all non-nationals know prior to taking up residence in the state that they are excluded from the vote, and this prohibition 'is enforced with absolute impartiality and procedural fairness' (Lovett 2010, p. 17), their exclusion from the vote would not be arbitrary.[11]

Now, access to political participation can have *instrumental* value in furthering non-domination in the context of social relationships. If the lack of the right to vote enables one person or a group to 'shape the various opportunities and constraints under which people (themselves or others) live out their lives' (Lovett 2010, p. 91), and thus the room for independent action available to them in social relationships, it would undermine non-domination in both the public and private sphere. Including non-nationals in the political rights of citizenship would thus be required to fulfil the principle of non-domination; not necessarily, however, as an immediate effect of taking up residence in the state. I will return to this point below.

Non-domination and the stairway to citizenship

I have made the case that our principle of non-domination requires for its practical fulfilment, first, that certain procedural constraints on the exercise of people's social power in the context of social relationships be in place, and second, that the social disadvantages which attach to a formal status are not such that the holders of that status will choose to trade away their freedom from domination to secure some basic need, or become dependent on the charity of someone else to meet those needs. However, substantial *equality* between citizens and resident non-nationals, with respect to material goods and rights, is not necessary to protect against domination as defined here. Furthermore, equal democratic standing is required, but only when deemed necessary as an instrumental measure to protect against practices of domination in social relationships.

However, I want to argue that a principle of non-domination would nonetheless require that the degree of inclusion into the privileges of citizenship increase gradually over time. It would require, borrowing a more visual term, that resident non-nationals be able to walk a 'stairway' towards citizenship (Engelen 2003), where each echelon gives access to a bundle of new citizenship rights and privileges. As non-nationals step onto higher echelons over time, their rights and privileges vis-à-vis the state, citizens and other non-nationals residents would, on this model, expand. The state's obligation to expand the set of citizenship rights available to resident non-nationals over time is based on the presumption that in order to fulfil the principle of non-domination in practice, the state has a prima facie obligation to reduce domination in *all* its forms and degrees. There are forms and degrees of domination that are more severe or basic than others, and from which it is more important to protect people. Presuming that liberal democratic societies value, and are therefore committed to reducing, practices of domination, but that they have limited resources with which to fight all forms of domination at all time, I also presume that they would prioritize protecting resident non-nationals against the most severe forms of domination, domination 'at the margins' to borrow Lovett's phrase. However, with time, the state is required to also protect resident non-nationals from other, albeit less severe, forms of domination in order to fully realize the principle of non-domination in practice.

The claim that certain forms and degrees of domination are more severe than others hinges on an account of why domination is bad in the first place. For the purposes of my argument here I borrow Lovett's notion that domination is bad because it 'presents a serious obstacle to human flourishing', understood as 'success in achieving autonomously formulated, reasonable life plans, through [...] community with others, over a complete life' (Lovett 2010, p. 131). I further assume that domination can undermine a person's ability to autonomously formulate his or her life-plans in various ways, including through direct harms of exploitation and coercion, the harm of constantly engaging in strategic anticipation that the dominating party *could* exercise her social power even if it never occurs, the harm of unpredictability and constant precaution, and the harm of disrespect and self-contempt. A person subject to domination may experience only one or some of these harms, or not experience them at all. What is significant for our argument here is that these harms come in different degrees, depending on the strength of the various elements that constitute domination: dependence on the social relationship, the difference in social power between the parties to a social relationship of domination, and the degree of arbitrary exercise of power possible. A person can be more or less dependent on a social relationship, the difference in social power can be smaller or larger, and the scope of unchecked, or arbitrary exercise of social power left to the agent of domination by legal rules and regulations and so forth can vary (Lovett 2010). A social relationship in which the subject's exit cost is exceedingly high, combined with a large difference in social power and lack of formal rules regulating the more powerful agent's exercise of that power is one in which the subject's ability to autonomously formulate his or her life-plans is practically absent. By contrast, a social relationship in which the exit cost is high but not unbearable for the subject, where the difference in social power is not great, and there are certain rules in place to regulate the difference in that power is one in which the subject's ability autonomously to formulate his or her life-plans is restricted although not completely so. The principle of non-domination as defined here permits that we prioritize fighting the forms of domination that are most threatening to people's ability to autonomously formulate their life plans, but then require that we *add* rights over time, to protect against forms or degrees of domination that are less threatening to persons' ability to do so, with the aim to reducing domination in all its forms and degrees, including the less severe ones.

As I see it, vulnerability to the most severe forms and degrees of domination is at its strongest for newly arrived residents, whose level of integration into society is presumably low. A first stage of inclusion of resident non-nationals would thus aim at preventing the most severe forms and degrees of domination to which a person can be subject. We would also aim at this stage to reduce the chances that the dominated party in this social relationship would choose to trade away his freedom from domination in exchange for material goods to meet fundamental needs, such as food, clothes, shelter, and health treatment. Neither of these two aims would require that the person be granted *all* rights upon taking up residence. Rather, a basic set of rights would be justified in order to keeping the most severe forms of domination at a constant low.

With time non-residents become more permanent, establish social networks, learn some of the language, become more informed about their rights, which contribute to making them less vulnerable to the most severe forms of domination. However, they may come to be in social relationships in which they are vulnerable to other, less severe forms and degrees of domination. As time passes, other, measures intended to prevent less severe forms and degrees of domination in social relationships should therefore be introduced, adding to the measures already implemented at the first stage.

With time, the person should also be given the opportunity to affect the background conditions that largely determine the various opportunities for and constraints on independent action available to them in social relationships. As we have seen, our principle of non-domination does not tie the justifiability of non-nationals' statuses to immediate equal democratic standing. However, it would nonetheless require incremental access to the sites of political decision-making over time to prevent others using their political power to shape the background conditions for action in a way that undermined non-nationals' room for independent action in social relationships, beginning for instance with the workplace and the neighbourhood, and ending at the national level.

We can thus picture a first level non-national status that gives newcomers access to the full range of civil rights, access to the labour market, as well as to public entitlements to cover some, though not necessarily all, basic needs, such as clothes, shelter and healthcare. As Engelen puts it, this would not only 'shield against the arbitrary use of state power' but would also 'protect against arbitrary interferences by citizens and other residents' (Engelen 2003, p. 509). Moreover, it would make non-citizens economically independent. Finally, it would also 'protect them against biological impediments to work' (p. 509), although not against the vagaries of the market (e.g. redundancies).

A second level of non-national status would include rights and entitlements that protect against dependence on public officials' and private persons' good-will to help or assist. On the third level non-nationals would be given access to the pension system and unemployment benefits, as well as voting rights in the workplace to protect against vagaries of the market, and further reduce the social power of the employer. On the fourth level there would be an opening for access to democratic participation at the local and regional level. At a fifth and final level, resident non-nationals would be given the opportunity to naturalize and thus gain access to participate in national elections.

As I see it, only some version of unequal residence statuses for resident non-nationals modelled on the idea of a stairway to citizenship can accommodate both the inclusive and exclusive commitments integral to the concept of liberal democratic citizenship. This model of differentiated inclusion into the rights of citizenship also corresponds with the actual practice of various forms of 'semi-citizenships' for non-nationals in contemporary liberal democracies (Cohen 2009). Moreover, in line with citizenship's commitment against subordination, the principle would also ensure that, regardless of the echelon that a non-national has reached on this stairway, the legal and social disadvantages that attach to her formal status would never become so great that it enabled state officials, private citizens or other non-nationals to use their social power over her arbitrarily, or make her dependent on private persons' charity to meet her basic needs.

A concept of freedom understood as non-domination arguably avoids the problems with the equality and rights approaches: it requires equality in the trivial sense that everyone subject to the state's power is worthy of having their liberty (understood as freedom from others' purposes) respected. Equality in this sense is equal freedom from domination. However, it avoids the demands of egalitarianism, which as we have seen, is not compatible with the exclusivist dimension of citizenship. Freedom from domination does not demand equal access to public goods and services; only the minimum required to enable the person to withstand relationships of domination. Non-domination also avoids the problem of indeterminacy that characterizes the rights discourse. Instead, it provides a way of delimiting that to which the individual have a claim against the state. The language of rights is helpful in articulating these claims, but cannot ground them.

Conclusion

I have sought to construct an account of justifiable forms of non-national statuses in the context of liberal democratic society, taking as my starting point the inclusive and exclusive normative dimension of the concept of citizenship, of which the status of non-national semi-citizenship is both a confirmation and a denial. Non-national status confirms that of citizenship because citizenship is an attribute of membership and so gains some of its meaning only with reference to a population of non-nationals. But non-national status is also a denial of citizenship because it represents everything that citizenship is not, or aspires not to be. Assuming the justifiability of excluding non-nationals at the territorial border, which is the exclusive dimension of citizenship in its purest form, I reflected on the possibility of arriving at a principle for the regulation of resident non-nationals that can accommodate both the inclusive and the exclusive aspects of the concept of citizenship. I took these aspects of citizenship to represent normative, and therefore, justifiable orientations integral to contemporary liberal democracies. Presuming that a principle must exhibit a reasonable balance of these conflicting orientations to qualify as valid, I set out to construct a principle that could accommodate both. In so doing I looked to values seen as integral to the concept of citizenship for guidance, notably those of equality, individual rights and freedom, which I defined in terms of non-domination. I argued that the latter is preferable to the other two, on the basis that its practical realization would accommodate both the exclusive and the inclusive dimension of the liberal democratic concept of citizenship, the reason being that it requires no more than a *partial* inclusion in the privileges of citizenship upon first admission to residency, but then requires that the degree of inclusion for resident non-nationals increase gradually, over time. At the same time, the model of differentiated residence statuses for resident non-nationals that the principle of non-domination sanctions fits with the idea reflected in liberal democracies' actual practice of a step-by-step inclusion in citizenship over time.

Acknowledgements

Work on this paper began during my stay at the University of Wales, Newport, in 2010 as a Leverhulme Overseas Research Fellow. I owe a special thanks to Phillip Cole for the many helpful discussions of the paper during my time there. An earlier version of the paper was presented at the 'Non-Citizens in Liberal Democracies – Republican and Liberal Perspectives' workshop held at Newport, March 2011. Many thanks to the participants for their constructive comments. Particular thanks to my discussant Enzo Rossi. I also owe special thanks to Iseult Honohan for very instructive comments on later versions of the paper; and two anonymous referees.

Notes

1. Various groups of nationals may also lack some of the rights of citizenship, including children (who lack the right to vote), the mentally ill (who lack the right to vote), military personnel (who may only be permitted to stand trial in military courts), and lesbian, gay, bisexual and transgendered (who may not be permitted to marry). The question of the justifiability of these forms of semi-citizenships is beyond the scope of this paper.
2. Several contributions to the relevant literature skip the question of which rights resident non-nationals should enjoy on their way to full inclusion, and focus instead on the question of when and why resident non-nationals should be granted full citizenship (e.g. Walzer 1983, Carens 1989, 2010, Smith 2008, Seglow 2009, Shachar 2009, Cohen 2010).
3. To borrow John Rawls's infamous term (Rawls 1971).
4. For illuminating historical and current examples of this practice of 'jus tempus', see Cohen (2010).
5. Other examples in the relevant literature of the use of a contextualist method include Benhabib (2004), Shachar (2001) and Shapiro (1999).
6. Tourists and other visitors are not considered here, as they are not normally considered residents of the state.
7. Of course, absent the non-ideal circumstances that this paper assumes, exclusion does not follow logically from the concept of citizenship, since, as one anonymous reviewer points out, it is possible at the level of ideal theory 'to make sense of a proposal for a world state of which everyone is awarded citizenship'. Since the argument in this paper is not conducted at the level of ideal theory, I do not pursue that point further here.
8. Strictly speaking it is not the principle of human rights that is doing the work in Carens's approach to the question of which rights resident non-nationals should enjoy, but a combination of liberal democratic states' own understanding of morally acceptable living and working conditions in society's different spheres and the principle of equal treatment. However, arguably the problem of indeterminacy appears also on this reading, as there is no non-arbitrary way of separating the spheres in which resident non-nationals should be treated equally, from the spheres in which the principle of equal treatment does not apply.
9. Lovett's definition of domination and non-domination differs from that of other definitions in the relevant literature in several respects. It is beyond the scope of this paper to discuss these differences here, but see, for example, Wartenberg (1990), Pettit (1997), and Shapiro (1999, 2012).
10. For a view to the contrary, see Goodin (2003), Carter (2008) and Kramer (2008).
11. Contrast this *procedural* interpretation of arbitrary use of social power with a *substantive* interpretation, according to which social power is arbitrary when used without regard to the interests of the affected parties. For this latter interpretation of arbitrariness, see, for example, Pettit (1997).

Notes on contributor

Marit Hovdal-Moan is a postdoctoral research fellow at the Philosophy Department, Norwegian University of Science and Technology (NTNU), Trondheim. Her research focuses primarily on normative approaches to international migration management, and the moral justifiability of state borders and boundaries. Her latest publication is 'Borders as a space of interaction: an account of special state obligations to irregular immigrants', *American behavioural scientist* (2012).

References

Barbalet, J.M., 1988. *Citizenship: rights, struggle and class inequality*. Milton Keynes: Open University Press.

Bauböck, R., 1994. *From aliens to citizens: redefining the status of immigrants in Europe*. Aldershot: Avebury.

Bellamy, R. and Palumbo, A., 2010. *Citizenship*. Farnham: Ashgate.

Benhabib, S., 1996. *Democracy and difference: contesting the boundaries of the political*. Princeton, N.J.: Princeton University Press.

Benhabib, S., 2004. *The rights of others: aliens, residents, and citizens*. Cambridge: Cambridge University Press.

Benn, S., 1967. *Egalitariansim and equal consideration of interest*. Nomos: IX, 67–78.

Bobbio, N., 1990. *Liberalism and democracy*. London: Verso.

Bosniak, L., 2006. *The citizen and the alien: dilemmas of contemporary membership*. Princeton, N.J.: Princeton University Press.

Brubaker, R., 1992. *Citizenship and nationhood in France and Germany*. Cambridge, Mass.: Harvard University Press.

Carens, J.H., 1989. Membership and morality: admission to citizenship in liberal democratic states. *In*: W.R. Brubaker, ed. *Immigration and the politics of citizenship in europe and north america*. Lanham, MD: German Marshall Fund and University Press of America.

Carens, J.H., 2000. *Culture, citizenship, and community: a contextual exploration of justice as evenhandedness*. Oxford: Oxford University Press.

Carens, J.H., 2002. Citizenship and civil society: What rights for residents? *In*: P. Weil and R. Hansen, eds. *Dual nationality, social rights and federal citizenship in the US and Europe: The reinvention of citizenship*. Oxford: Berghahn Books, 100–118.

Carens, J.H., 2008a. Live-in domestics, seasonal workers, and others hard to locate on the map of democracy. *The journal of political philosophy*, 16, 419–445.

Carens, J.H., 2008b. The rights of irregular migrants. *Ethics & international affairs*, 22, 163–186.

Carens, J.H., 2010. *Immigrants and the right to stay*. Cambridge, Mass: MIT Press.

Carter, I., 2008. How are power and unfreedom related? *In*: C. Laborde and J. Maynor, eds. *Republicanism and political theory*. Oxford: Blackwell, 58–82.

Cholewinski, R., 2004. *The legal status of migrants admitted for employment: a comparative study of law and practice in selected European states*. Strasbourg: Council of Europe Publishing.

Cohen, E.F., 2009. *Semi-citizenship in democratic politics*. Cambridge: Cambridge University Press.

Cohen, E.F., 2010. Jus tempus in the magna carta: the sovereignty of time in modern politics and Citizenship. *PS: Political science & politics*, 43, 463–466.

Cole, P., 2000. *Philosophies of exclusion: liberal political theory and immigration*. Edinburgh: Edinburgh University Press.

Costa, M., 2009. Neo-republicanism, freedom as non-domination, and citizen virtue. *Politics, philosophy & economics*, 8, 401.

Cranston, M., 1973. *What are human rights?* London: The Bodley Head.

Engelen, E., 2003. How to combine openness and protection? Citizenship, migration, and welfare regimes. *Politics & society*, 31, 503–536.

Fiss, O.M., 1999. *A community of equals: the constitutional protection of new Americans*. Boston: Beacon Press.

Galloway, D., 2008. Noncitizens and discrimination: redefining human rights in the face of complexity. *In*: O. Schmidtke and S. Ozcurumez, eds. *Of states, rights, and social closure: governing migration and citizenship*. New York: Palgrave MacMillan, 37–59.

Goodin, R.E., 2003. Folie républicaine. *Annual review of political science*, 6, 55–76.

Gunsteren, H.R.V., 1998. *A theory of citizenship: organizing plurality in contemporary democracies*. Boulder, Colo.: Westview Press.

Heater, D., 1999. *What is citizenship?* Cambridge: Polity Press.

Howard, M.M., 2009. *The politics of citizenship in Europe*. Cambridge: Cambridge University Press.

Jones, P., 1994. *Rights*. London: Macmillan.

Kagan, S., 1998. *Normative ethics*. Boulder: Westview Press.

Kramer, M.H., 2008. Liberty and Domination. *In*: C. Laborde and J. Maynor, eds. *Republicanism and political theory*. Oxford: Blackwell, 31–57.

Lovett, F., 2010. *A general theory of domination and justice*. Oxford: Oxford University Press.

Miller, D., 2000. *Citizenship and national identity*. Cambridge: Polity Press.

Miller, D., 2008. Irregular migrants: an alternative perspective. *Ethics & international affairs*, 22, 193–197.

Pettit, P., 1997. *Republicanism: a theory of freedom and government*. Oxford: Clarendon Press.

Pocock, J.G.A., 1995. The idea of citizenship since classical times. *In*: R. Beiner, ed. *Theorizing citizenship*. New York: State University of New York Press, 29–52.

Rawls, J., 1971. *A theory of justice*. Oxford: Oxford University Press.

Sangiovanni, A., 2007. Global justice, reciprocity, and the state. *Philosophy and public affairs*, 35 (1), 3–39.

Santoro, E., Bellamy, R. and Castiglione, D., 2004. *Lineages of European citizenship: rights, belonging and participation in eleven nation-states*. Basingstoke: Palgrave Macmillan.

Seglow, J., 2009. Arguments for naturalisation. *Political studies*, 57, 788–804.

Shachar, A., 2001. *Multicultural jurisdictions: cultural differences and women's rights*. Cambridge/New York: Cambridge University Press.

Shachar, A., 2009. *The birthright lottery: citizenship and global inequality*. Cambridge: Mass., Harvard University Press.

Shapiro, I., 1999. *Democratic justice*. New Haven: Yale University Press.

Shapiro, I., 2012. On non-domination. *University of toronto law journal*, 62, 293–336.

Shue, H., 1996. *Basic rights: subsistence, affluence, and U.S. foreign policy*. Princeton, N.J.: Princeton University Press.

Skinner, Q., 1998. *Liberty before liberalism*. Cambridge: Cambridge University Press.

Smith, R.M., 2008. Birthright citizenship and the fourteenth amendment in 1868 and 2008. *University of Pennsylvania journal of constitutional law*, 11, 1329.

Soysal, Y.N., 1994. *Limits of citizenship: migrants and postnational membership in Europe*. Chicago: University of Chicago Press.

Walzer, M. 1983. *Spheres of justice: a defense of pluralism and equality*. New York: Basic Books.

Wartenberg, T.E., 1990. *The forms of power: from domination to transformation*. Philadelphia: Temple University Press.
Whelan, F.G., 1983. Prologue: democratic theory and the boundary problem. *In*: J. Chapman, ed. *Nomos*. New York and London: New York University Press, 13–47.
Young, I.M., 1990. *Justice and the politics of difference*. Princeton, N.J.: Princeton University Press.
Young, I.M., 2007. *Global challenges: war, self-determination and responsibility for justice*. Cambridge: Polity Press.

Republicanism and the constitution of migrant statuses

David Owen

Politics and International Relations/Centre for Citizenship, Governance and Globalisation, University of Southampton, Southampton, UK

This paper addresses republican conditions of legitimacy for the constitution of the civic statuses of migrants. It identifies two legitimacy tests to which any civic status is subject, namely, that it does not make its bearers more vulnerable to the arbitrary exercise of private or public power (R1) and that the constitution of the person as bearer of this status is not itself the product of an arbitrary exercise of public power (R2). It is argued that R1 puts significant constraints on what can be legitimate migrant statuses and R2 links republicanism to cosmopolitanism in terms of a basic norm in respect of the production and allocation of civic statuses in that those who are subject to such a regime should have the effective power to 'shape and contest' the rules of this regime.

Introduction

It is a feature of our contemporary political societies that those who populate them may have distinct civic statuses: 'citizen', 'permanent resident', 'temporary worker' and 'irregular migrant' are all general classes of such civic statuses, each of which has more specific variants within it. For example, in the context of European Union member states, the general status-class 'citizen' comprises 'resident citizen', 'absentee citizen' and 'permanent non-resident citizen', where the latter encompasses 'non-resident citizen resident within the European Union' and 'non-resident citizen resident outside the European Union'. All these civic statuses – general or particular – can be, and typically are, characterized by distinct ensembles of rights and duties, where the contemporary order of global governance is such that, with limited qualifications, the authority to constitute and vary such statuses is held by states (or by judicial or governmental structures constituted and authorized by states such as the European Union). Yet contemporary republican political theory (Pettit 1997, Honohan 2002, Richardson 2002, Bellamy 2007) is characterized by a focus on relations between citizens and barely attends to the question of the constitution of citizenship as a status, let alone the plethora of other civic statuses that populate our political domain. This is surprising since many of the more obvious forms of what prima facie appear as exemplary instances of domination concern migrants. This paper attempts to redress this lacuna by addressing the value of republicanism for reflecting on the legitimate constitution of such statuses.

Power, domination and civic statuses

Civic statuses can stand in two main relationships to the exercise of power over subjects:

- A status may enable (or obstruct) the exercise of power over the status-bearer by private or public actors.
- A status may itself be the outcome of an exercise of power over the person (individual or collective) constituted through this exercise of power as the bearer of this status.

Republicanism is, however, focused on domination, that is, on the arbitrary exercise of power over persons (individual or collective) rather than the exercise of power over persons as such.[1] Hence, from a republican standpoint, the normative significance of civic statuses can be expressed thus:

> R1. A status may enable (or obstruct) the arbitrary exercise of power over the status-bearer by private and/or public actors.

> R2. A status may itself be the outcome of an arbitrary (or non-arbitrary) exercise of power over the person (individual or collective) through which the person is constituted as bearing the status.

We can think of R1 and R2 as distinguishing two tests that a civic status must satisfy. Thus, R1 directs us to the question of whether someone who is characterized by a particular civic status is in virtue of that fact exposed to arbitrary exercises of private and/or public power, while R2 directs us to the question of whether the imposition of a given civic status on a person itself constitutes an arbitrary exercise of public power. The claim advanced in this article is that a republican regime is fully legitimate on its own terms if and only if those subject to its rule are not subject to domination in either of the senses picked out by R1 or R2.

To give this normative outlook any purchase on political issues, however, requires that we specify the relevant sense of an arbitrary exercise of power. In this paper I start from a procedural view according to which what links R1 and R2 is the issue of whether the exercise of power over subjects is justifiable in terms that they can rationally and reasonably accept as free and equal persons who stand to one another in relationships specified by particular normative contexts. An initial gloss on justifiability in this context might run thus:

> an exercise of power is justifiable in terms that those subject to it can rationally and reasonably accept as free and equal persons if it supports the agent's autonomy and/or well-being.

However, this initial formulation is open to what appears to be a powerful objection that points out that the reference to 'autonomy and/or well-being' entails that this formulation can support paternalist interventions in which a focus on well-being may override the agent's autonomy. To consider this objection, and how it may lead us to reformulate these modes, we can attend to some cases of prima facie legitimate public paternalism, where an action is paternalist if, and only if, it intentionally, or reasonably foreseeably, usurps the judgment of the other party, and thereby deliberately or effectively attributes a non-autonomous status to the other party.

The first cases are those in which the attribution of a non-autonomous status to the relevant agents is justified, that is, cases involving agents who lack autonomy such as the seriously mentally impaired and children. In the case of children, we may plausibly argue that interventions to support their well-being are generally only legitimate if they also support, or at least do not obstruct or undermine, the development of their autonomy. In the case of those who are damaged such that the attainment (or recovery) of autonomy is not a plausible prospect, it may seem clearer that public paternalism is justified, but even here it is notable that our practice often involves 'proxies' who are seen as standing in special relationships to the mentally incompetent person and are presumptively able to make judgements that *either*, in some counterfactual sense, track the judgments that the incompetent person would have made (this is most plausible in the type of case exemplified by adult children acting on behalf of parents who have become mentally infirm) *or* express a focused concern with their well-being that should not be lightly disregarded (e.g., parents of children born with severe mental disability).

The second cases are those concerned with fairly systematic failures of reasoning by human beings in general; failures that have been the locus of discussion in the recent literature on choice architectures and nudges where the concern is with exploiting or, more kindly, harnessing the ubiquity of such reasoning failures to support the future or overall autonomy and/or well-being of agents. A classic example is arranging state pensions as 'opt out' rather than 'opt in' in the full knowledge that people are both liable to reasoning failures with respect to the autonomy and well-being of their future selves compared to their present selves and less likely to opt out than opt in. Hence, more people are likely to be better protected if an 'opt out' system is adopted. This arrangement of choice architecture is best viewed as 'autonomy-compromising' rather than 'autonomy-breaching' since it does not attribute a non-autonomous status but rather a qualified autonomous status to persons. As in the previous cases, however, it would appear to be a reasonable constraint on such form of 'soft paternalism' that they can only be candidates for legitimacy insofar as they harness those reasoning failures that cannot plausibly be overcome (at least not without this being unduly costly or burdensome)[2] in order to support the future autonomy of those subject to the choice architecture in question.

On the basis of these reflections we can reformulate the key component of the specification of these modes of drawing the arbitrary/non-arbitrary distinction by replacing the phrase:

> an exercise of power is non-arbitrary if it supports the agent's autonomy and/or well-being

with this alternative formulation:

> an exercise of power is non-arbitrary if it supports the agent's autonomy or supports their well-being without either breaching their autonomy or compromising their autonomy in ways that do not also enhance their future or overall autonomy.

At this stage, a second query is liable to arise, namely, how we can best determine whether an exercise of power is non-arbitrary in this sense, i.e., what institutions do we need to secure confidence that our judgments of non-arbitrariness will reliably track non-arbitrariness.

We can distinguish three types of institution that can plausibly take on this task: epistemic institutions of expert knowledge, legal institutions of judicial review, and political institutions of democratic decision-making. It may be objected that only political institutions can be justified as an institutional arrangement for distinguishing arbitrary and non-arbitrary exercises of power since there is a central difference between political institutions, on the one hand, and epistemic and judicial institutions, on the other. In political institutions, those who are subject to the exercise of power collectively constitute the authority that will decide whether to engage in this exercise of power. In epistemic and judicial institutions, authority is invested in an independent third party and hence does not fully respect the autonomy of those subject to the exercise of power. This line of objection, namely, that epistemic and judicial institutions are themselves paternalist, follows naturally from autonomy-based conceptions of political justice such as that proposed by Rainer Forst (2007/2011), but it also gains support from politically realist approaches to constitutionalism such as that developed by Richard Bellamy (2007), which stress the propensity of epistemic and judicial institutions to serve as sources of the arbitrary exercise of power. These are significant considerations and give us prima facie reason to privilege political institutions within a political system but not, I think, to disavow the value of epistemic and judicial institutions as elements within a fair political process that act as partial checks on the quality of that process. I will return to this point in the final section of this paper.

R1-Legitimacy and civic statuses

What is the relevant context for considering R1 in relation to the civic statuses of migrants? In introducing this section, I want to explain why 'the state' considered in isolation is not a satisfactory response to this question. One way to see this is to notice that the extent to which a civic status held in one state enables or obstructs the arbitrary exercise of power over the bearer of that status may depend in part on the civic status enjoyed by that person in another state. Thus, for example, someone who holds the status of 'permanent resident' in state A may be differentially exposed to arbitrary exercises of private or public power in this state depending on whether they also have citizenship in good standing in another state B. This is so simply because permanent residents who are stateless or who initially entered as refugees (and where the conditions that caused their flight continue) do not enjoy, *de jure* or de facto respectively, the external citizenship rights of automatic re-entry and diplomatic protection that permanent residents who are citizens in good standing with another state do enjoy, and the absence of these rights is liable to mean that they are more vulnerable to the arbitrary exercise of at least some forms of private or public power. (It is also the case that the value and effectiveness of these external citizenship rights varies across different sending and receiving states, and the relationships between them, in ways that may differentiate even those permanent residents who do enjoy citizenship in good standing in their state of nationality.) Another example that helps to illustrate the salience of the transnational context is the general status of 'British national,' which comprises six distinct civic statuses incorporating transnational elements: British citizenship, British overseas citizenship, British overseas territories citizenship, British national (overseas), British protected person and British subject. Notably, whereas it was once the case that any British subject had the right to reside in the UK, it is now only those holding the first status and some of those holding the last who are entitled in virtue of their status (in the first case) and their status combined with some specified qualifying conditions (in the last case) to live and work in the UK.[3] In this respect, as Bauböck (1994, 2003, 2005, 2009; see also Owen 2012) has long argued, the default context for consideration of R1 is the transnational context in which migrants are situated as having civic statuses in two (or more) states (a point that is partially, but only partially, recognized in the International Convention on the Protection of the Rights of All Migrant Workers and Members of their Families).[4]

We can, following and augmenting Bauböck (2003, 2007), distinguish five general types of transnational civic status:

- Denizens who are citizens of one state but lawful residents of another and, in virtue of such residence, have one of a range of possible civic statuses (other than citizenship) in the state of residence: permanent resident, temporary worker, etc. (A special case of denizenship verging on dual citizenship is that of European Union citizens who reside in a member state that is not their state of nationality.)
- Dual (or plural) nationals who have nationality in two (or more) states where the terms of their nationality may vary (as in the case of British nationality) and, in typical cases where nationality entails citizenship, the terms of their citizenship may vary in terms whether they are, legally speaking, resident, temporary absent or permanently absent.
- Ethnizens who are citizens of one state but share an ethnocultural identity with the members of a different (typically neighbouring) state in virtue of which they enjoy a civic status in relation to that state (e.g., a right to accelerated naturalisation if they move or a right to cultural subsidies if they remain in their state of legal nationality).
- Refugees and stateless persons to whom the state of residence stands *in loco civitatis* (Owen 2014) in virtue of the fact that these residents either lack a nationality or are not able effectively to enjoy the rights that pertain to their nationality.
- Irregular migrants who are citizens of one state and are de facto present in another for residence and/or working purposes but do not have a legal entitlement to be so (and hence have what we might call a 'negative civic status' in the state in which they are present).

In considering the position of persons with transnational civic statuses, I will distinguish between their exposure to arbitrary exercises of private and public power. I will not in this context consider each type separately, as I have elsewhere (Owen 2013), but will focus on the main forms of domination to which they are exposed, referring to the different types when it helps to bring specific issues into focus.

Since a person who has civic statuses in two states may, in virtue of that fact, be exposed to – or, in the case of dual citizens, protected from – arbitrary exercises of private and public power in each of these distinct sites of power, I will structure this discussion by addressing the two sites of sending state and receiving state.

Sending states

With the exception of stateless persons and, in effect, refugees, the relevant normative relationship in which to consider emigrants and their exposure to arbitrary exercises of power in their home states is that of national citizenship. From a republican standpoint, it is part of the point and purpose of the institution of citizenship to protect those who legitimately hold this status from arbitrary exercises of private and public power, that is, exercises of power that are not justifiable to those subject to it in terms that they can rationally and reasonably accept as free and equal persons who stand to one another as equal members of a self-governing polity. This establishes a normative basis for both human rights (as free and equal persons) and civil, political and social rights (as equal members of a self-governing polity) in the context of a judicial system structured in terms of the rule of law. It is part of the point of being a citizen that one is not dependent on the good will of private or public actors for the security of one's rights and welfare. In this respect, emigrant citizens are entitled to the same protection of their human and civic rights as resident citizens. It is important to note that the mere fact of absence from the territory of the state does not imply that they do not have rights-protected private interests (and, for that matter, duties) within the home state in respect of, for example, property (broadly construed) that they own in the state or the way in which their own welfare is bound up with the welfare of their family. Nor does it imply that they do not retain rights and duties with respect to their public interests in the home state of both general (e.g., its maintenance as a free state) and specific (e.g., as primary agent responsible for their security, rights and welfare) kinds. This latter point is most obviously illustrated by the right to diplomatic protection when abroad, but it extends beyond this to a state's duty to ensure that its emigrant citizens are treated by the receiving state in ways that are compatible with respect for their human rights and the rights basic to the normative relationships of resident and/or worker that they inhabit in the receiving state. The home state has a general duty to protect its citizens from arbitrary exercises of private and public power, and while the institutional mechanisms through which it does so will necessarily be different in respect of emigrant citizens than resident citizens, the fact that it is constrained to discharge this duty through diplomacy, treaties, and other indirect mechanisms should not be taken to imply that the duty is any less binding on the state in the case of emigrant citizens since they are, after all, citizens.

Taking the issue of private interests first, consider that the republican focus of equal freedom from domination involves a concern not merely with the nominal possession of rights but with the effectiveness of rights for all citizens as bulwarks against domination. Thus, for example, if it is the case that the poor are unable to enjoy equal effective protection of their rights as the wealthy, this represents a legitimacy problem from a republican standpoint, and addressing this problem involves a focus on generating institutional mechanisms that ensure, as far as practically possible, in terms that can be rationally and reasonably be justified to citizens (i.e., where doing so does not breach basic rights or impose what they justifiably take to be undue costs on the citizenry considered collectively or severally), such equal effective protection. A distinguishing feature of the poor is their lack of private resources for ensuring the protection of their rights that can, in part, be addressed through institutionally securing, for example, a publically funded police force and the widespread availability of high quality legal representation through legal aid or required *pro bono* work. The same normative point applies in the case of emigrants whose distinguishing feature is their absence from the state. This absence renders them more vulnerable to domination in contexts in which the institutional mechanisms through which the state protects rights presupposes as a background norm that rights-bearers are present and where this presumption of presence is consequential with respect to the state's expectations concerning the costs of identifying and reporting prima facie rights-violations and its articulation of the obligations of citizens in this respect. The basic point here is that state mechanisms for protecting the rights and welfare of citizens have understandably been developed in the context of a general presumption of the presence of the citizen within the territory of the state and may not be well-adapted to protecting their rights and welfare in their absence without, for example, the activity of an agent with the power to act legally on behalf of the emigrant and, further, since the activity of such agents (where they turn out to be untrustworthy) may itself be a source of private domination, the legitimate claims to rights and welfare of emigrant citizens should be understood not simply as entailing duties on the part of the state to protect the 'home state' rights and welfare of emigrants but as generating specific obligations to ensure that it has the appropriate mechanisms in place to ensure the *equal* protection of the rights and welfare of emigrant citizens relative to resident citizens.[5] This might include, for example, regular checks by welfare agents to confirm that the family of the typically male emigrant are not being subject to abuse or exploitation in virtue of the fact that the husband/father is absent.[6]

What of the exposure of the emigrant to the arbitrary exercise of public power by the home state? For republicans, part of the importance of citizenship is as an institution through which the exercise of public power can be both authorized and held to account such that citizens are not subject to discretionary forms of power and, hence, are not dependent on the good will of state officials or politicians in respect of their legitimate rights and welfare. The primary mechanisms through which authorization and accountability are secured being citizens' rights of political participation and their rights to engage in judicial contestation of administrative and political decision-making. Thus, the key issue here concerns the way in which the absence of the emigrant from the territory of the state may intersect with their citizenship in these respects. Empirically, we can note a number of important respects in which the citizenship of emigrants often differs from that of residents (Bauböck 2007, Owen 2011).[7] First, emigrants may not enjoy the same political rights as residents, thus, for example, voting rights as well as rights to found, join and fund political parties in the home state may be considerably more restricted or even excluded. Second, there is the issue of potential loss of citizenship in virtue of the acquisition of another citizenship through one's residence in another state that arises for emigrant citizens but not resident citizens. Third, even where they enjoy some rights of political participation, emigrants may lack institutional routes through which to participate effectively in the politics of their home state to ensure the protection of their legitimate interests as citizens and, more specifically, as emigrant citizens. Fourth, external rights of citizenship have particular importance for emigrant citizens but access to, and the exercise of, these rights are typically mediated through engagement with state officials in embassies, consulates and the ministry dealing with foreign affairs where the possibility and/or burdens of initiating a process of judicial contestation located in the home state may be quite different to those applying to the contestation of administrative decisions applicable to residents.

The latter two differences raise issues analogous to those concerning equal protection in respect of arbitrary exercise of private power and generate specific obligations on the state to develop institutional mechanisms for ensuring equality; however, the first and second differences require separate treatment since we cannot presuppose that such variations are R1-illegitimate. Rather, we need to ask whether these differences between resident citizens and emigrant citizens can be rationally and reasonably endorsed by these citizens as elements of the institution of citizenship. Thus, for example, a number of theorists hold that it is relevant to such deliberations to note that emigrant citizens are not comprehensively subject to the legal regime of their home state in the way that resident citizens are or, again, that being resident outside the state, emigrant citizens do not have to bear the costs of many domestic policies (Lopez-Guerra 2005, Rubio-Marin 2006, Bauböck 2007, Owen 2010, 2011). Whether or not such variation in civic status can be R1-legitimate hangs on whether the legitimate interests of emigrant citizens as citizens and as emigrants can be effectively protected from arbitrary exercises of public power in ways that are compatible with such differences.

It is helpful first to make a distinction between what, for current purposes, we can call 'constitutional law' and 'regulatory law'. Constitutional law, as concerned with the basic terms and conditions of the political association, is constitutive of the legal personality of, and binding on, all citizens. Regulatory law, as concerned with guiding the conduct and structuring the relationships of all persons subject to the jurisdiction of the polity, is, in the case of states, typically binding on those who are territorially present within its authoritative jurisdiction. (Regulatory law need not be limited in its scope to the territory of the state but its effective extension beyond the state's territory requires cooperation with other states or transnational actors.) This distinction is helpful in two respects. First, it clarifies the point that any alteration in the terms of citizenship generally or of the status-relationship between resident citizens and emigrant citizens in particular is a constitutional issue in which all citizens, irrespective of their place of residence, have a legitimate interest (see also Owen 2011). Second, it focuses the point that, while emigrant citizens may have legitimate interests in relation to regulatory law (e.g., if they retain property or family in the state), such law (1) pertains primarily to residents and (2) the general interests of emigrants in respect of regulatory law, namely, the equal protection of human and civic rights, are continuous with the interests of residents. In relation to variation in the rights of political participation of resident and emigrant citizens, these points suggest that some variation could be rationally and reasonably endorsed by citizens if certain basic conditions were in place to ensure that the legitimate interests of emigrant citizens (considered severally) were given equal weight with those of resident citizens. Thus, for example, a plausible candidate for legitimacy would be a regime that included commitment to the mandatory inclusion of *all* citizens in constitutional referenda, rights of border-crossing free political speech, protest and association for emigrant citizens, an Ombudsman to represent the interests of emigrant citizens in policy-making, and rights of appeal to a contestatory court where emigrants can contest legislation that they hold does not, despite the efforts of the Ombudsman, give impartial consideration to their legitimate interests.

What of the potential loss of citizenship on acquisition of a further nationality? Such a law would be constitutional in our sense and hence require the assent of citizens (resident and emigrant), but could they rationally and reasonably agree to such a principle? There are two main reasons for thinking that such a principle would be reasonably rejected. Consider, first, that a republic has an interest in the development of a civic bond between citizens such that citizens regard their membership as non-instrumentally valuable. This is important because it supports civic solidarity and an orientation to the common good. In other words, the instrumental value of the state for its citizens as a regime protecting them from domination may hang on enough of its citizens valuing the state for non-instrumental reasons. The state will typically seek to cultivate this relationship and outlook through the education of its citizens and the institutions in and through which they interact as well as, more broadly, through its civic culture. In this way, the state plays a central role in constituting the identities of its citizens (Smith 2008). But, as a consequence, emigrant citizens who experience their relationship to their home state as non-instrumentally valuable have a legitimate interest in retaining citizenship of this state. The second reason is given by the empirical observation that many emigrants now have lives that are increasingly transnational in character, often involving regular movement between home state and state of residence or participation in dense social networks that span the states in question and which would be severely disrupted by loss of home citizenship (Rubio-Marin 2006). While it is justifiable to require duties of emigrant citizens including a regular reaffirmation of their relationship to the home state, such considerations suggest that the imposition of loss of citizenship on acquisition of a new citizenship would constitute an arbitrary exercise of public power.

Receiving states

If we turn to consider the context of the receiving state, the relevant normative relationships are (as just mentioned) those of being a resident and/or a worker (typically, at least in aspiration, both) and, hence, from a republican standpoint, justification of varying civic statuses concerns whether they can be rationally and reasonably endorsed by free and equal persons who stand to one another in these relationships, where to pass the threshold of being a candidate for justification requires that a civic status secures human rights and those rights basic to the relationship of resident and/or worker.

What, though, are the rights basic to the relationship of residents and/or workers? Given the central focus of republicanism on the value of non-domination combined with the coercive power of the state with respect to its own territorial jurisdiction, rights basic to the relationship of residents must include effective rights to act civically *qua* resident, that is, to report abuses of human and civic rights, to draw attention to the ways in which a status renders its bearer liable to what one takes to be arbitrary abuses of private and public power, to engage in free speech, free association and political protest. Effective enjoyment of such rights necessarily requires that one's residence (regular or irregular) is not compromised by the exercise of these rights.

What of rights basic to the relationship of workers? These include effective rights to work in conditions governed by rules of health and safety, and of fair remuneration that pertains impartially to any worker undertaking the labour in question, as well as rights of civic activity *qua* worker, such as rights to form and join a union, to change one's employment, to engage in legitimate forms of employment protest and of political protest concerning one's rights as a worker. Effective enjoyment of such rights necessarily requires that one's employment is not compromised by the exercise of these rights.

These conditions of justification effectively rule out a range of specific variants within civic statuses such as 'temporary worker' as R1-illegitimate, most obviously, for example, civic statuses defined by work visas that make one's entitlement to residence dependent on working in a specific job for a specific employer, since, to adapt Skinner (1998, p. 41), while such an employee may as a matter of fact be able to act at will, they remain at all times *in potestate domini* (for a pertinent liberal critique of such visa regimes, see Carens 2008a). It is a regrettable fact that we have all too many examples of such conditions of contemporary servitude, most obviously with respect to those who work in household contexts.[8] These legitimacy conditions also place significant constraints on the conditions under which a negative civic status such as 'irregular migrant' can plausibly be an R1-legitimate status, since they require the construction of firewalls such that knowledge of their civic status that is acquired by public officials through the exercise of their rights (not least the exercise of their rights to protect themselves against forms of private domination) cannot be used against the agent in question in any determination of their right to residence in much the same way that knowledge acquired through illegal searches cannot be used against the individual subject to the search (for defences of firewalls, see Bosniak 2006, Carens 2008b). This point does not deny that the state has a legitimate interest in tracking 'irregular migrants', it simply limits the means through which the state can pursue this interest by insisting that the democratic state's commitment to the freedom and equality of all persons present in the state as bearers of human rights has lexical priority over that interest.

But we should also draw attention to a further issue that was brought to widespread attention by Michael Walzer's (1983) argument that guest workers are subject to 'citizen tyranny', namely, subjection to laws and policies which they have no voice in determining, and which, Walzer argued, required easy access to citizenship as the appropriate mode of protection against such a condition of domination. Although effective recourse to human rights and the rights basic to resident and workers do ameliorate the extent of the citizen tyranny to which Walzer directs our attention, they do not fully resolve the problem, and in this respect the issue of access to citizenship for residents must be a pertinent republican concern. At this juncture, issues of transnationalism and variations in transnational status also return to the fore.

Consider, first, that the citizen tyranny argument does not entail immediate enfranchisement of resident non-citizens, since we can reasonably draw a distinction between 'transient' and 'permanent' residents, where the former legitimately retain full political rights, including voting rights, in their home state on the presumption that they are temporary absentees, while the latter legitimately may not enjoy identical political rights in their home state to those citizens who reside there on the presumption that they are permanent non-residents. How should the distinction between transience and permanence be drawn? Two points seem pertinent. The first is coordination of the distinction across states so that the period of transient absence (from the point of view of home state) and of transient presence (from the point of view of receiving state) are the same. (It is preferable that such coordination is omnilateral to avoid differentiation between immigrants resident in a given receiving state who come from different home states and between emigrants from a given home state who are resident in different receiving states.) The second is that where the distinction is drawn should give due attention to both relevant empirical and normative factors. Thus, for example, it is empirically relevant to note that the rate of return of migrants to their home state declines over time such that it is unlikely that migrants who have stayed for more than seven years will return during their working lives, while it is normatively relevant to note that, in a representative democracy characterized by regular elections, we pragmatically accept that individual citizens may be unable to vote for a period in which they have voting rights because of when the elections fall (hence if the voting age is 18 and my 18th birthday falls one day after the national election, it may be typically 4–5 years before I can exercise my right to vote in national elections).

Such considerations suggest that the European Union average of 5 years as marking the distinction between 'transient' and 'permanent' is a reasonable position. However, and this is where variations in transnational status enter the frame, this distinction is not pertinent to the cases of stateless persons and refugees who lack political rights in another state, and this normatively salient fact supports the claim that they should enjoy rather more accelerated access to citizenship – nor is it pertinent in the same way to those on serial temporary visas insofar as they serially retain full political rights in the home state or to irregular migrants where, in both cases, longer periods of time may be justifiable (Owen 2013).

Finally, we should note that the reasons that suggest that a home state would be acting illegitimately in withdrawing the citizenship of an emigrant on their acquisition of a new citizenship also entail that a receiving state would be acting illegitimately if it required the surrender of citizenship of the home state as a condition of acquiring its citizenship. There are both normative and pragmatic reasons for this claim. The pragmatic reason is that rates of naturalization and integration are higher if immigrants are not required to surrender their prior nationality. The principled reason is that such a requirement places an unreasonable burden on immigrants given that their relationship to their state of origin is typically of both instrumental and non-instrumental value to them.

Summary

The focus of this section on R1-legitimacy has addressed that ways in which bearing a civic status may render individuals vulnerable to arbitrary exercises of private and public power and, more significantly, how to address and specify the kinds of conditions that a civic status must meet to enjoy R1-legitimacy by attending to the relationships that give substance to the procedural account of legitimate (non-arbitrary) exercises of power that I have adopted. But coming to bear a given status is itself the product of an exercise of power by sending and/or receiving states, and this directs us to the significance of R2-legitimacy in which we focus on the conditions under which the production and attribution of civic statuses can be rationally and reasonable endorsed by free and equal persons who are subject to this civic status regime.

R2-legitimacy and civic statuses

We can distinguish *general* and *restricted* civic status regimes. By the phrase 'general civic status regime', I refer to the regime composed of the assemblage of rules and norms – domestic, regional, international, transnational – through which all human beings are assigned general civic statuses such as national citizen of A, dual national of A and B, national citizen of A and European Union citizen, resident non-citizen, stateless person, refugee, etc. – *and* through which the authority and power to vary access to, and the content of, such civic statuses is distributed. With the phrase 'restricted civic status regime', I refer to the motley of rules and norms through which authorized agents (primarily states) vary access to, and the specific content of, such general statuses and produce particular civic statuses as members of these general statuses (e.g., types of nationality or types of resident non-citizen).

The general regime is produced, maintained and transformed through the actions and interactions of states supplemented by a range of other judicial and political agents. A given restricted regime is produced, maintained and transformed through the actions and interaction of a state with a range of other judicial and political agents (including other states). Are those subject to the general and specific civic statuses produced in this way subject to domination?

To address this question, consider Arash Abizadeh's (2008) recent work on border controls which, he rightly notes, coerce not merely members but also non-members, and which he argues, consequently, require for their democratic legitimacy that all who are subject to coercion are entitled to form the demos that determines border laws. Abizadeh's argument is a democratic rather than a specifically republican one, but one can offer a republican variant on it: border controls represent an invasive interference with the freedom of choice of people in general in that they close off or attach specific (typically burdensome) conditions to taking up certain choices; as such both border controls in general and specific border regimes in particular require that, for such controls to be legitimate (non-arbitrary), those subject to them can rationally and reasonably endorse them as free and equal persons who stand in a relationship of common subjection to them. There are two points to note here.

The first is that border controls are an exercise of public power predicated on distinguishing between persons on the basis of their civic statuses (most obviously, between citizens and non-citizens but also, within the latter category, between permanent residents, refugees, tourist and temporary workers, etc.) and, hence, presupposes the legitimacy of allocating different civic statuses to persons. More generally, border controls are simply one of many types of exercise of public power supported by the current order of global governance and articulated in specific forms through particular states that are so predicated on distinguishing between persons in terms of civic statuses attributed by states (collectively or severally) to them. Abizadeh's argument focuses on a special case of a much more general phenomenon.

The second point concerns what would be required for the production and imposition of civic statuses to be a non-arbitrary exercise of public power, i.e. for general and specific civic status regimes to be legitimate. We can notice here that republicanism requires at least one civic status: citizen. We can plausibly add that republicanism insofar as it is acutely concerned to avoid concentrations of power is likely to support (barring exceptionally compelling reasons of the kind that might be generated by such phenomena as nuclear proliferation or climate change that concern the very survival of humanity) a world of plural polities and, hence, a distinction between citizens and non-citizens. How is this distinction to be worked out in terms of rules of acquisition and loss of citizenship/non-citizenship beyond a strict requirement that all human beings should always have effective membership of at least one polity? Republicanism does not offer a unique institutional solution to this issue of determining the general civic status regime (although it certainly articulates constraints and guidelines) and, consequently, the question arises of who is to decide on the character of such a regime. On the procedural view of distinguishing arbitrary and non-arbitrary exercises of power that I favour, the answer to this question is necessarily all those who are governed by it. In this respect, republicanism entails political cosmopolitanism. Notice, however, that this does not *entail*, in the way that Abizadeh's argument does, the constitution of a global demos through global cosmopolitan institutions, although it is compatible with such an institutional proposal. For an exercise of public power to be legitimate, what is required is that those who are subject to it, considered collectively and severally, can effectively shape and contest this exercise of public power – and while one way, perhaps the best way, of constituting a public with the effective power to shape and contest the exercise of public power is to do through the construction of inclusive democratic institutions, this is not the only way of securing this power of legitimation. The same point applies in the case of restricted civic status regimes. These are, as we have noted, subject to a range of constraints and amongst such constraints are requirements that allow those subject to these regimes to engage in forms of political protest concerning the character of the regime or regimes in question. Although, by itself, this is too weak to satisfy the test of effective power to shape and contest, it does point in another possible direction. Notice that we might take the distinction between 'general' and 'restricted' civic status regimes to be significant and argue for global cosmopolitan institutions to rule the general regime but adopt alternative measures with respect to restricted regimes. This would require normative and empirical work to specify the best feasible options. My point here is simply that the fact the republicanism entails political cosmopolitanism does not in and of itself entail global cosmopolitan institutions.

In summary, the imposition of a civic status is an arbitrary act of public power unless all subject to such imposition have the effective power to shape and contest. Notice though that 'shape and contest' should be read together, the criterion is not that those subject to a regime should have an effective power to shape and a separate effective power to contest the regime in question (although this may be the best option) but that they should have an effective power to 'shape and contest' the regime. In this respect, the distribution of this power may vary across 'shaping' (active/formative) and 'contesting' (reactive/reformative) dimensions. This is important because it implies that it may be legitimate that some persons enjoy very little power to shape the exercise of public power (e.g., simply rights of cross-border speech and protest) if at the same time they have significant power to contest the exercise of public power. (It should be noted though that the relationship is asymmetrical to the extent that the 'shaping' of public power is institutionally organized as a collective process in a way that, importantly for securing non-domination, need not be true of the 'contesting' of public power).

Republicanism, democratic rule and institutional design

The preceding discussions of R1 and R2 legitimacy acknowledge an important point about republican political theory, namely, its concern not simply with norms and principles but with the choice and effects of the institutional structures through such commitments are realized. This is nicely illustrated in, for example, Richard Bellamy's bracing critique of non-majoritarian democratic practices, which argues that the defence offered of such institutions of delegated governance in terms of their deliberative character and their subjection to judicial review fails to recognize that both mechanisms are potential sources of arbitrary rule before robustly concluding in support of majoritarian democratic rule that 'the only legitimate and effective way to ensure that all citizens are treated with equal concern and respect is to have procedures that provide them with equal power to make their rulers responsive and accountable to their rights and interests' (Bellamy 2008, p. 186). Yet Bellamy's argument is predicated on addressing a context in which the residents of a state are wholly citizens and the citizens of the state are wholly resident. This is, however, nowhere the case. To discharge their duties to emigrant citizens and to immigrant non-citizens, states are likely to have to engage in forms of institutional innovation or recourse to mechanisms that may be less robust than majoritarian democracy, but which are more feasible in the political circumstances that we currently inhabit.

It is relatively straightforward to point to examples of state innovation in respect of emigrant citizens and immigrant non-citizens. Thus, for example, we can note that the norm of single nationality has decisively collapsed. While not yet a constitutionally protected right in states, more than 100 states now accept, or at least tolerate, dual nationality, and the trend towards allowing this status has accelerated significantly over the past 20 years. Thus, in 1996, about 40 states officially allowed dual nationality. By 1998 the number had grown to 55, and by 2001 the number had grown further to 93 (Kivisto and Faist 2007). Drawing on the work of Sejersen (2008), we may now add at least another 10 states. A similar story can be told about the increasingly widespread recourse of states to the political incorporation of emigrant citizens by way of expatriate voting rights, as Table 1 demonstrates.

The third trend of state innovation is considerably less spectacular and marks the gradual development of, typically, local electoral rights for resident non-citizens. The current position is summarized in Table 2.

My point in referring to these developments is not to claim that they are motivated by the normative concerns of republican theory, but rather to illustrate that states are increasingly alert to, and innovating in response to, the issues posed by global migration, not least through the institution and transformation of transnational civic statuses attested to by these trends.

Table 1. Countries with voting rights for non-resident citizens.

Region (n)	Polity
Africa (24)	Algeria, Angola, Benin, Botswana, Cape Verde, Central African Republic, Chad, Ivory Coast, Djibouti, Equatorial Guinea, Gabon, Ghana, Guinea, Guinea-Bissau, Mali, Mozambique, Namibia, Niger, Rwanda, São Tomé and Príncipe, Senegal, Sudan, Togo, Tunisia
Americas (16)	Argentina, Bolivia, Brazil, Canada, Columbia, Dominican Republic, Ecuador, Falkland Islands, Guyana, Honduras, Mexico, Nicaragua, Panama, Peru, United States, Venezuela
Asia (16)	Afghanistan, India, Indonesia, Iran, Iraq, Israel, Japan, Kazakhstan, Kyrgystan, Oman, Philippines, Syria, Tajikistan, Thailand, Uzbekistan, Yemen
Europe (40)	Austria, Azerbaijan, Belarus, Belgium, Bosnia and Herzegovina, Bulgaria, Croatia, Czech Republic, Denmark, Estonia, Finland, France, Georgia, Germany, Gibraltar, Greece, Guernsey, Hungary, Iceland, Italy, Jersey, Latvia, Lichtenstein, Lithuania, Luxembourg, Isle of Man, Moldova, Netherlands, Norway, Poland, Portugal, Romania, Russia, Slovenia, Spain, Sweden, Switzerland, Turkey, Ukraine, United Kingdom
Pacific (10)	Australia, Cook Islands, Fiji, Marshall Islands, Micronesia, Nauru, New Zealand, Palau, Pitcairn Islands, Vanuatu
Total = 106	

Note: Adapted from IDEA (2007), tables 1.2, 1.4.

The capacity of republican political theory to guide our reflections in relation to these forms of innovation is that because it combines a focus on the basic norm that those subject to rule should be able effectively to shape and contest such rule with attention to the institutions through which the shaping and contesting of rule is given expression, it provides resources for evaluating such innovations both individually and collectively. Here we can usefully return to Bellamy who, in concluding his defence of political constitutionalism, acknowledges that his general argument confronts a challenge in cases of 'discrete' minorities. His examples are asylum seekers and the Roma. Bellamy argues that 'the exceptional character of this sort of case cannot provide an all-purpose argment for judicial review' (Bellamy 2007, p. 258). This is a fair claim. However, two points should be noted. First, the issue of 'discrete minorities' may be rather less exceptional than Bellamy contends if it encompasses the full range of those holding migrant civic statuses and, thus, there may be a greater place for judicial review in addressing issues of R1 legitimacy than Bellamy acknowledges. This is especially significant in contexts where we have good reasons for thinking that the quality of political judgment is low when tested against our best epistemic standards, and that it may be low because there are political incentives for powerful actors to maintain that state of affairs. Second, in the context of the political requirement of R2 legitimacy that those subject to public power should be able effectively to shape and contest the exercises of power to which they are subject, judicial review has an

Table 2. Countries with electoral rights for resident non-citizens.

	Restricted	Universal
National	Australia Barbados Belize Guyana Ireland St. Lucia St. Vincent and Grenadines Trinidad and Tobago United Kingdom Portugal	New Zealand Malawi Chile Uruguay
Regional or local	European Union (27 member states) Canada Israel	Ireland Denmark Finland Iceland Norway Sweden Belgium Luxembourg Netherlands Estonia Hungary Lithuania Slovakia Slovenia Belize Venezuela (Bolivia) (Columbia)

Note: Adapted from Bauböck (2005), p. 684.

important role as a compensatory mechanism for those whose 'shaping' power is legitimately more limited than resident citizens. These considerations also support the view that the epistemic and judicial institutions can play a pertinent role with a fair political process in directing our attention to contexts and cases where there is a significant gap between the views of justifiable exercises of power that emerge from epistemic or judicial institutions on the one hand, and political institutions on the other hand. The point here is not that the epistemic or judicial institution has priority over the political institution in tracking arbitrariness but rather that they alert us to contexts and cases where we have prima facie reason to scrutinize the fairness of the political process.

At the same time, though, Bellamy's argument against legal constitutionalism as a general outlook also helps alert us to the importance of what Seyla Benhabib (2006) refers to as 'democratic iterations', that is, the way in which democratic autonomy and cosmopolitan right can be reconciled through the demos of a state transforming itself into accordance with cosmopolitan norms.

In the context of republican concerns about the concentration of power, it is perhaps best to see epistemic and judicial institutions as elements within the wider process of democratic iteration than as competitors to it.

Conclusion

This paper has identified two legitimacy tests to which any civic status is subject, namely, that it does not make its bearers more vulnerable to the arbitrary exercise of private or public power (R1) and that the constitution of the person as bearer of this status is not itself the product of an arbitrary exercise of public power (R2). The second of these legitimacy requirements is often effectively occluded by the tendency of republican theorists to focus on citizenship and the state such that even the question of the constitution of citizenship – of who is entitled to it and under what terms and conditions – is treated as an unproblematic given. To overcome this tendency, this article has sought both to show why the issue of diverse civic statuses matters and to draw attention to the resources of republican political thought for addressing it. I have argued that the basic norm in respect of the production and allocation of civic statuses is that those who are subject to such a regime should have the effective power to 'shape and contest' the rules of this regime, where it is important to note that although democratic governance may be the best general way of realizing this public power to shape and contest, it is not the only way nor always the best in particular circumstances, and that this is itself a reason to build epistemic and juridical institutions into the political process. I have argued that a republican account of legitimate civic statuses need not, in the way that a democratic account does, entail global cosmopolitan institutions; it is compatible with such a world, but it is also compatible with a world of plural polities enmeshed in processes of democratic iteration – or, indeed, with a combination of the two. The purpose of this paper is, not least, to draw attention to the importance of such issues and to open a discussion on these institutional questions.

Acknowledgments

I am grateful to Iseult Honohan for her editorial support and comments; and to an anonymous referee for saving me from an embarrassingly careless slip as well as for other sensible suggestions. I also owe thanks to the other participants at the 'Republicanism and Migration' conference held at Newport. Although this paper bears almost no relation that which I gave at the conference, the day's discussion with Iseult Honohan, Enzo Rossi, Meghan Benton, Chris Bertram, Marit Hovdal Moan and others has remained in my mind and formed something of the spur to write the present paper.

Notes

1. Central contemporary republican texts include Bellamy (2007), Pettit (1997, 2012), Skinner (1998), Richardson (2002), Laborde and Maynor (2008), Laborde (2008), and Lovett (2010).

2. Of course, what counts as 'unduly burdensome' is open to political interpretation, and this may matter in ways that are consequential.
3. For current specifications of these statuses, see http://www.ukba.homeoffice.gov.uk/britishcitizenship/othernationality/britishsubjects/ [Accessed 31 January 2013].
4. http://treaties.un.org/Pages/ViewDetails.aspx?src=TREATY&mtdsg_no=IV-13&chapter=4&lang=en [Accessed 31 January 2013).
5. In contexts in which the sending state lacks the capacity and/or disposition to do so, there is an obligation on its citizens to reshape the state and, in circumstances where the citizenry lack the capacity and/or disposition to transform the state appropriately, on the international community to build the capacity of either the citizenry or of the state and/or to shape the disposition of the citizenry or of the state.
6. This situation is more complicated in contexts in which the emigrants are refugees who have fled their state of nationality (or previously habitual residence), because, in contrast to economic emigrants who are members in good standing with the home states (and with respect to whom states typically have prudential reasons to protect their 'home' rights and welfare based not least on the value of remittance flows to their economies), refugees have fled state persecution (or persecution by private actors from whom the state could not or did not protect them). Here international mechanisms are required, such as robust requirements on the state of refuge to facilitate family reunification.
7. It is notable that this is a rapidly changing field of state practice and policy, as I illustrate below in the final section of this paper.
8. For a recent news report on this issue in the UK, see http://www.guardian.co.uk/lifeandstyle/2010/aug/06/domestic-workers-slaves [Accessed 31 January 2013].

Notes on contributor

David Owen is Professor of Social and Political Philosophy at the University of Southampton. He has published nine books and numerous articles on a wide variety of topics. He is currently writing books on migration and on Nietzsche.

References

Abizadeh, A., 2008. Democratic theory and border coercion: no right to unilaterally control your own borders. *Political theory*, 36 (1), 37–65.

Bauböck, R., 1994. *Transnational citizenship*. Cheltenham: Edward Elgar.

Bauböck, R., 2003. Towards a political theory of migrant transnationalism. *International migration review*, 37 (3), 700–723.

Bauböck, R., 2005. Expansive citizenship – voting beyond territory and membership. *Political science and politics*, 38 (4), 683–687.

Bauböck, R., 2007. Stakeholder citizenship and transnational political participation: a normative evaluation of external voting. *Fordham law review*, 75 (5), 2393–2447.

Bauböck, R., 2009. The rights and duties of external citizenship. *Citizenship studies*, 13 (5), 475–499.

Bellamy, R., 2007. *Political constitutionalism*. Cambridge: Cambridge University Press.

Bellamy, R., 2008. Republicanism, democracy and constitutionalism. *In*: C. Laborde and J. Maynor, eds. *Republicanism and political theory*. Oxford: Basil Blackwell, 159–189.

Benhabib, S., 2006. *Another cosmopolitanism*. New York: Oxford University Press.

Bosniak, L., 2006. *The citizen and the alien*. Princeton: Princeton University Press.

Carens, J., 2008a. Live-in domestics, seasonal workers, and others hard to locate on the map of democracy. *Journal of political philosophy*, 16 (4), 419–445.

Carens, J., 2008b. The rights of irregular migrants. *Ethics and international affairs*, 22 (2), 163–186.

Forst, R., 2011. *The right to justification*. New York: Columbia University Press.

Honohan, I., 2002. *Civic republicanism*. London: Routledge.

IDEA. 2007. *Voting from abroad* [online]. Available from: http://www.idea.int/publica tions/voting_from_abroad/ [Accessed 1 March 2013].

Kivisto, P. and Faist, T., 2007. *Citizenship: discourse, theory and transnational prospects*. Oxford: Wiley-Blackwell.

Laborde, C., 2008. *Critical republicanism*. Oxford: Oxford University Press.

Laborde, C. & J. Maynor eds. *Republicanism and political theory*. Oxford: Basil Blackwell.

Lopez-Guerra, C., 2005. Should expatriates vote? *Journal of political philosophy*, 13 (2), 216–234.

Lovett, F., 2010. *A general theory of domination and justice*. Oxford: Oxford University Press.

Owen, D. 2010. Resident non-citizens, non-resident citizens and voting rights. *In*: G. Calder et al. *Citizenship acquisition and national belonging*, Basingstoke: Palgrave, 52–73.

Owen, D. et al. 2011. Transpolitical citizenship. *In*: G. Stoker et al. *Prospects of citizenship*. London: Bloomsbury Academic, 110–133.

Owen, D., 2012. Transnational citizenship and the democratic state. *Critical Review of Social and Political Philosophy*, 14 (5), 641–663.

Owen, D., 2013. Citizenship and the marginalities of migrants. *CRISPP*, 16 (3), 326–343.

Owen, D., 2014. *In loco civitas*: on the normative structure of the international refugee regime. *In*: S. Fine and L. Ypi, eds. *Migration in political theory*. Oxford: University Press, forthcoming.

Pettit, P., 1997. *Republicanism*. Oxford: Oxford University Press.

Pettit, P., 2012. *On the people's terms*. Cambridge: Cambridge University Press.

Richardson, H., 2002. *Democratic autonomy*. Oxford: Oxford University Press.

Rubio-Marin, R., 2006. Transnational politics and the democratic national-tate: normative challenges of expatriate voting and nationality retention of emigrants. *New York university law review*, 81, 117–147.

Sejersen, T.B., 2008. 'I vow to thee my countries' – the expansion of dual citizenship in the 21st Century. *International migration review*, 42 (3), 523–549.

Skinner, Q., 1998. *Liberty before liberalism*. Cambridge: Cambridge University Press.

Smith, R. 2008. The principle of constituted identities. *Ethics and global politics*, 1 (3). Available from http://www.ethicsandglobalpolitics.net/index.php/egp/article/view/1860. Accessed on 1/2/2013.

Walzer, M., 1983. *Spheres of justice*. New York: Basic Books.

Immigration, interpersonal trust and national culture

Lubomira Radoilska

Philosophy, University of Cambridge, Cambridge, UK

This article offers a critical analysis of David Miller's proposal that liberal immigration policies should be conceptualized in terms of a quasi-contract between receiving nations and immigrant groups, designed to ensure both that cultural diversity does not undermine trust among citizens and that immigrants are treated fairly. This proposal fails to address sufficiently two related concerns. Firstly, an open-ended, quasi-contractual requirement for cultural integration leaves immigrant groups exposed to arbitrary critique as insufficiently integrated and unworthy of trust as citizens. Secondly, the focus on national culture instead of citizenship obfuscates the close link between political membership and political trustworthiness. An examination of two models of interpersonal trust, affective and cognitive, shows that there is no room for the mid-way position associated with a quasi-contract. The effect of grounding political trust in a shared national culture instead of democratic institutions is to normalize the domination of immigrants and citizens alike.

Is sharing a national identity necessary for interpersonal trust in a democratic welfare state? If so, what are the implications of this for the task of defining a cogent set of liberal immigration policies? More specifically, should immigrant groups be expected to integrate into existing national cultures, and what is the best way to conceptualize this expectation? The present article elucidates these issues by offering a critical analysis of David Miller's recent proposal, according to which liberal immigration policies should be conceptualized in terms of a quasi-contract between receiving nations and immigrant groups. This quasi-contract is designed to ensure that cultural diversity due to mass immigration does not undermine trust among citizens whilst at the same time immigrants are treated fairly. It will be argued that Miller's proposal fails to address sufficiently two related concerns. Firstly, by being open-ended, a quasi-contractual requirement for cultural integration exposes immigrant groups to arbitrary critique for being insufficiently integrated and so unworthy of trust as citizens of their adopted countries. Secondly, by focusing on national culture instead of citizenship, Miller's proposal inadvertently makes political membership appear secondary to culture in the discussion of political trustworthiness. To support this conclusion, I examine two major models of interpersonal trust – affective and cognitive trust – and I show that there is no room for a mid-way position consistent with a notion of a quasi-contract. I then identify and explore an important effect of grounding political trust in a shared national culture instead of democratic institutions: to normalize the domination of immigrants and citizens alike.

Miller on immigration and political trustworthiness

In his article, 'Immigrants, nations, and citizenship', Miller (2008) identifies the big question about immigration as:

> whether citizenship alone is a sufficiently strong cement to hold together a democratic welfare state, whose successful working depends upon relatively high levels of interpersonal trust and co-operation, or whether it is also necessary for the citizens to share a cultural identity of the kind that common nationality provides. (p. 378)

Building on earlier works (Miller 1995, chs 4–5, Miller 2000, ch. 4), Miller argues for the second position; citizenship as political membership is insufficient alone to guarantee social cohesion within a democratic welfare state. With respect to immigrants, this position seems to imply further requirements, in addition to obeying the laws of the state they join and accepting the basic principles of liberal democracy which underlie its public life. These requirements are meant to ensure that immigrants integrate within the existing national culture to a degree that allows them to partake in a shared identity with the native-born citizens. The objective is to avoid the dilution of interpersonal trust, which Miller considers to prevail in culturally divided societies where support for a democratic welfare state is generally weakened, and which is particularly problematic in the case of redistributive policies across cultural or ethnic lines. Drawing on evidence from the United States and some other multicultural democracies (Miller 2008, pp. 379–380), Miller suggests that the cultural integration of immigrants is essential if liberal democracies are to maintain their commitment to upholding the social rights of citizenship. For, if some immigrant groups are seen as poorly integrated within the national culture, the rest of the citizens will be reluctant to support redistributive policies that would benefit these groups. The thought seems to be that, by staying out of the mainstream culture, not only would immigrants make themselves untrustworthy *qua* citizens in the eyes of the national majority, this would also contribute to the overall weakening of the fabric of society.

Miller is quick to point out that his argument does not assign a merely passive role to immigrants. He writes: 'In arguing that immigrants should be expected to integrate culturally and accept elements of the existing national culture, I do not mean to exclude their contribution to the reshaping of that culture, a process that happens in any case, but ideally should do so through open debate between different sections of the national community' (p. 387). This is consistent with the underlying ambition of his project, which is to find a mid-way between two contrasting positions on immigration within liberalism, the one focusing exclusively on the idea of national sovereignty and the other on the human rights of the immigrants (p. 389). This ambition is expressed in the idea of a quasi-contract between the citizens of the receiving state and new immigrant groups, which according to Miller should be fair to both sides (pp. 371–372). Miller discusses and rejects three main categories of arrangements that benefit the receiving nation at the expense of immigrants: first, an expectation that immigrants completely assimilate to the cultural patterns of the society they join; second, the selection of immigrants on grounds of their ethnicity or perceived cultural proximity; and third, the default treatment of immigrants as untrustworthy. An example of the first category is the so-called 'Tebbit test' demanding that 'immigrant groups from Commonwealth countries cheer for the English team and not for their countries of origin when watching cricket matches' (p. 372). The second category is illustrated by a survey of popular attitudes to immigration in the Netherlands indicating that the majority would favour a cultural fit criterion for new immigrants, which Miller considers to be implicitly reliant on a 'too-rigid conception of national culture' (p. 388). Finally, the arrests of people of German origin in the UK and people of Japanese origin in the United States during the Second World War are instances of the third category, default treatment of immigrants as untrustworthy by the state. According to Miller, these instances were particularly prejudicial since 'many of those interned were in fact strongly committed to their adopted countries, and equally antagonistic to the countries they left' (p. 383). Thus, by reflecting on the wrongness of state distrust levelled at trustworthy immigrants, Miller is able to make the following general point: 'The state should act toward immigrants on the basis that they are committed citizens, until in the case of any particular individual there is clear evidence to the contrary' (p. 383).

Could the mid-way position on immigration outlined by Miller avoid a default assumption that immigrants are untrustworthy citizens merely by virtue of being immigrants? This question is pressing since, at closer inspection, the three categories of cases where immigrants are allowed to join in on inequitable terms exhibit a common underlying structure. Both a requirement for complete assimilation to the national culture and a selection of immigrants on grounds of cultural proximity seem to reiterate, in their own ways, the response to immigration that is expressed in a default attitude of distrust. In a nutshell, this response can be put as follows: to the extent that immigrants are identifiable as such, as opposed to blending in, they are not an integral part of the nation. And so, the question: 'Whose side are they really on?' would seem to be acceptable to ask in a variety of situations, from the mundane to the critical, from the cricket pitch to the battlefield.

Admittedly, this is the kind of pitfall that Miller's conception of a quasi-contract between receiving nations and immigrant groups is meant to pre-empt.[1] For if a state is reluctant to acknowledge some groups as sufficiently integrated within the established culture unless they are also completely assimilated to it, this would create a powerful disincentive to their being committed citizens to this state. A good illustration of the attitude to beware of is offered by an episode in E. M. Forster's *A Passage to India* (1924). There, Ronny Heaslop remarks to Adela Quested on the subject of their mutual acquaintance, Dr Aziz:

> He shook his head laughing.
> 'Have I said anything funny?'
> 'I was only thinking how the worthy doctor's collar climbed up his neck.'
> 'I thought you were discussing the caves.'
> 'So I am. Aziz was exquisitely dressed, from tie-pin to spats, but he had forgotten his back-collar stud, and there you have the Indian all over [...].
> (Forster 1924, p. 82)[2]

Clearly, if the requirement that immigrants integrate culturally takes the form of fault-finding for not achieving the impossible – in the eyes of Ronny Heaslop, Dr Aziz will never be a perfect gentleman or 'one of us' – immigrants will be effectively prevented from sharing a national identity with native-born citizens. As a result, the social cohesion and levels of interpersonal trust required for a well-functioning democracy would be as fragile as in cases when no cultural integration is expected at all, over and above the minimal understanding of a country's public life that enables newcomers to respect its laws.

There are two features of Miller's position that might be seen as problematic in this respect. First, according to Miller, the requirement that immigrants integrate culturally – although normative – 'cannot be sensibly cast in legal form' (Miller 2008, p. 371). This conceptualization seems intuitively appealing; it flows directly from the notion of a *quasi*-contract between receiving nations and immigrant groups. Drawing on the literature concerning the ethics of trust (e.g. Baier 1986, Jones 1996), we can appreciate why a less than fully formalized kind of interaction might be considered as conducive to trust between parties: it provides them with space for the expression of goodwill toward one another. However, this effect is typical of already established trusting relationships. It tells us how to sustain such relationships, not how to initiate them. In the absence of a secure grounding, less than fully specified expectations might be experienced as deliberately vague and even oppressive: one can never be sure to have lived up to such expectations. If the requirement that immigrants integrate culturally is not spelled out so that everyone can be clear about whether this has been fulfilled or not, it is difficult to see how a sneering attitude like the one exposed by Forster in the character of Ronny Heaslop is to be avoided in the midst of the receiving nation. As I shall argue in the following section, failing to address this concern is likely to lead to a political circumstance of self-fulfilling distrust between national majorities and immigrant groups. If these majorities feel free to recast the boundaries between insiders and outsiders of the national culture at their discretion, immigrants are liable to find themselves casually treated as outsiders, irrespective of how committed citizens they are trying to be. It would therefore be unsurprising if some of them felt disaffected with a national identity that they do not seem to be firmly acknowledged as sharing, so that they are subject to challenge on this account at will. In turn, such disaffection would feed into the image of immigrants as potentially untrustworthy and uncommitted citizens.

Second, the quasi-contractual requirements levelled at immigrant groups are tied in with national identity rather than citizenship. To see why this is problematic, let us consider again the arrests of people of Japanese origin in the United States during the Second World War. The policy did not distinguish between new arrivals in the country and citizens, even native-born citizens of a particular ethnic background. By identifying them collectively as 'people of Japanese origin', the preventive mass detention, to which they were all subjected, demonstrated how insignificant the US citizenship many of them held was in the eyes of the US state. This goes to the heart of the problem: if political trustworthiness is grounded in sharing a cultural identity rather than membership in a political community, the defensible divide between citizens of the receiving nation and immigrant groups is likely to shift into a pernicious one, between dominant and marginalized groups of citizens. For it is hard to see how a process of cultural integration such as that advanced by Miller (2008) – learning the national language, some aspects of the nation's history and political culture (p. 380) – would counteract this pernicious outcome. As shown by the preventive detention of people of Japanese origin in the United States during the Second World War, the perception of a group as politically untrustworthy seems to be primarily targeted at a feature which identifies members of the group as different from the national majority: ethnic background, some religious or cultural practice. Whether they have integrated into the national culture in the sense specified by Miller's mid-way position seems immaterial in this respect. The very fact of having a group identity in addition to the national one seems sufficient to trigger this kind of suspicion. Just as the vagueness of integration requirements placed on immigrant groups by a quasi-contract with the receiving nation has the potential to place arbitrary constraints and to contribute to the arbitrary exclusion of citizens associated with these groups, so does the focus on national identity as opposed to citizenship. As Philip Cole observes:

> The citizens/subjects boundary is based on a distinction between activities, not people: those activities proper to the public sphere of political citizenship. The citizens/outsiders boundary is based on a distinction between people, but in practice it is policed through controlling activities: outsiders cannot participate in the public activities definitive of citizenship. This creates potential dangers for certain groups of full members of the community. As the boundaries between citizens/subjects and citizens/outsiders coincide, the way the external boundary is policed will have an impact on the way the internal boundary is policed. In effect, any group that shares characteristics with those identified as outsiders will themselves be in a vulnerable position. Their membership will be constantly questioned; they will be subjected to forms of surveillance from which other members are free; and their access to the public sphere of citizenship will become hazardous.
>
> (Cole 2010, pp. 5–6)

To recap, Miller's conception of a quasi-contract between receiving nations and immigrant groups raises two related concerns. The first is that, by being open-ended, the requirement for integration leaves immigrant groups open to arbitrary critique for being insufficiently integrated and untrustworthy citizens of their adopted countries. The second is that, by focusing on national culture and not citizenship, Miller's proposal inadvertently makes political membership appear as secondary to culture in the discussion of political trustworthiness. This is likely to lead to various kinds of arbitrary exclusion, whereby full members of the political community are deemed as untrustworthy citizens merely by virtue of sharing in a presumably foreign religious, ethnic, or cultural background.

Could Miller's conception address satisfactorily these two concerns? This question boils down to establishing whether the close link between a shared national identity and trust among fellow citizens gets right the relationship between trust and trustworthiness in public life. For if it doesn't, the requirement for cultural integration which this conception places on immigrant groups will turn out to be not merely inefficient, but counterproductive. To see which of the two the case is, we need to place Miller's account in the context of recent work on the nature and basis of interpersonal trust.

Nature and basis of interpersonal trust

It is important to note that the kind of trust Miller's account relies on is interpersonal rather than institutional. This is a theoretical choice. After all, it is not immediately apparent why public willingness to contribute to a welfare system should be seen as dependent primarily on fellow citizens trusting one another rather than the institutions of their state.[3] This is not a critical point, but a clarificatory point meant to explain the relevance of the discussion to follow. For the models of interpersonal trust upon which I shall draw have not been developed specifically for political contexts, but are more general. This is not methodologically inappropriate since Miller's conception of trust also reflects a broader range of cooperative interactions. As indicated earlier, on Miller's view, the need for high levels of interpersonal trust among fellow citizens arises because citizenship rights have a strong social component within a democratic welfare state. More specifically, the problem of trust between receiving nations and immigrant groups has to do with the fact that, on the one hand, citizenship 'entails an equal claim to public goods' and, on the other, 'immigrants bring with them new demands for public goods' (Miller 2008, p. 381). These new demands amount not only to more people having access to the same kind and level of public services. The creation of new public services might be also required. Examples include public subsidies for religious and cultural practices, such as sports that are prevalent within specific immigrant groups. A degree of cultural integration is therefore meant to forestall the perception that such groups come to take unfair advantage of a system of social cooperation put in place and maintained by the receiving nation. By integrating into the national culture, immigrants would not only show that they are committed citizens worthy of trust, they would also be able to take part in an open, democratic deliberation about the nature and scope of public goods, to which the people of their adopted country should have equal access. As this summary shows, Miller's account of trust is not distinctly political. Instead, it aims to resolve a general problem of social cooperation – potential free-riding – in a context that is political, the relationship between nations and immigrants. And so, to ascertain whether this account is successful, we need to articulate and critically examine the ways in which it conceptualizes the nature and basis of interpersonal trust. In this respect, two queries will be of particular import. Firstly, is Miller's account of trust best understood in affective or cognitive terms? Secondly, on this account, is trust supposed to track trustworthiness or, conversely, attract it? These alternatives are not mutually exclusive. As we shall see in the following discussion, some accounts of trust (e.g. Hardin 1991, Pettit 1995) succeed in bringing together aspects of the affective and cognitive models. Similarly, the relationship between trust and trustworthiness could in principle run both ways: trust seems to be well placed when it responds to, just as when it elicits, trustworthiness.

Affective versus cognitive approaches to interpersonal trust

Here is the basic structure of trust that will be assumed in the subsequent analysis:

> x trusts y to φ because of z
>
> *Or*:
>
> A trustor trusts a trustee to perform or refrain from performing an action or set of actions on the basis of some reasons.

Drawing on Annette Baier's analysis of trust as three-term relationship in her seminal paper 'Trust and antitrust' (1986), the proposed structure has the advantage of offering a meeting ground for alternative approaches. Accounts such as Jones (1996) and Thomas (1990) consider trust to be fundamentally an affective attitude. These accounts take the trustor's attitude toward the trustee as a person to be more significant than the trustor's epistemic relationship to the reasons that speak in favour, or indeed against, their trusting this person. Alternatively, accounts, such as O'Neill (2002a) and Holton (1994), which consider trust to be a kind of belief responsive to evidence, take the latter epistemic relationship to be more significant than the trustor's attitude toward the person of the trustee. To see more clearly what the stakes are in fleshing out an account of political trust in either affective or cognitive terms, let us briefly discuss some clear-cut examples of each approach and then return to Miller's proposal.

In 'Trust as an affective attitude', Karen Jones (1996, p. 4) defines trust as follows:

> trust is an attitude of optimism that the goodwill and competence of another will extend to cover the domain of our interaction with her, together with the expectation that the one trusted will be directly and favourably moved by the thought that we are counting on her.

This attitude of optimism seems inseparable from a kind of benign cognitive bias. As Jones puts it (p. 12):

> Trusting thus functions analogously to blinkered vision: it shields from view a whole range of interpretations about the motives of another and restricts the inferences we will make about the likely actions of another. [...] What in the absence of trust would be taken to be a reason for jealousy, for wary suspicion, or for action to protect my interests will not be so taken when there is trust. It is because the one trusted is viewed through the affective lens of trust that those who trust are – usually cheerfully, and often on the basis of the smallest evidence – willing to risk depending on the one trusted.

This feature of the affective model, linking trust to a benign cognitive bias, is taken a step further by Laurence Thomas, who argues for a robust distinction between trust and predictability. According to Thomas, the more certain we are that a person cannot fail to act in a particular way, the less able we become to trust her with respect to this behaviour (Thomas 1990, p. 247). This is because the point of interpersonal trust is not to make sure that people fulfil some specific obligations toward one another, but to offer a different and more compassionate way of living together. As Thomas points out (p. 249):

> when there is affectional trust between individuals, then they look to one another to diminish the misfortunes that they suffer, and it is irrelevant whether the misfortune is such that from an objective and universal standpoint anyone else in the position to help would incur a moral obligation to do so.

In so doing, Thomas articulates the close link between two sides of the affective model of trust, which at first blush might appear as independent: the relative insignificance of evidence for or against the trustworthiness of the trusted and a departure from a morality expressed in terms of rights and obligations. Having established this link, he concludes:

> a world where trust abounds – and so one where trust prevails between people across differences in ethnic and religious heritage and differences in phenotype – is one where people contribute to one another's flourishing by affirming each other's moral worth. (p. 250)

In contrast, trust and evidence of trustworthiness are meant to go hand in hand on a cognitive model. This is because on this alternative model trust fundamentally boils down to a judgement about the trustee's trustworthiness. As Onora O'Neill (2002a, p. 64) succinctly puts it when reflecting on the apparent crisis of trust in public life in the UK:

> A crisis of trust cannot be overcome by a blind rush to place more trust. Our ambition is not to place trust blindly, as small children do, but with good judgment. In judging whether to place our trust in others' words or undertakings, or to refuse that trust, we need information and we need the means to judge that information. To place trust reasonably we need to discover not only *which* claims or undertakings we are invited to trust, but *what* we might reasonably think about them.

From this perspective, if trust is either predicated upon, or leads to a cognitive bias, this would not be considered as benign, even less as a defining feature of trust. In fact, any mismatch between trust and evidence of trustworthiness is deemed as problematic as that between a belief and the available evidence in support of this belief. What is more, the problem at hand is conceived primarily as a cognitive failure on the part of the trustor rather than an ethical fault which may sometimes lie with the trustor, e.g. for failing to trust the trustworthy, but also with the trustee, e.g. for betraying or exploiting a person's trust. Given that one of the main issues raised by Miller's proposal is how to avoid the default treatment of immigrants as untrustworthy, let us focus on how a cognitive model of trust would tackle instances where trust is unreasonably refused to trustworthy others. According to O'Neill, such instances, including 'misplaced mistrust, unwarranted suspicion and misjudged refusal to trust, even where there is adequate – if inevitably imperfect – evidence of trustworthiness' represent variations of the so-called 'Cassandra problem' (O'Neill 2002b, p. 141). For Cassandra's prophecies, albeit always correct, were persistently ignored by the Trojans, ultimately at their peril. O'Neill illustrates this problem with public distrust levelled at research that involves testing on animals in the UK: not only is the practice strictly regulated, there is also sufficient evidence that lab animals are treated humanely, and it is made available to the public. Yet, this evidence is widely ignored and testing on animals is seen with suspicion, if not flatly condemned. To correct this kind of cognitive bias, O'Neill suggests that, instead of further transparency, a regime of intelligent accountability be implemented (O'Neill 2002a, pp. 41–59). This is because, once a Cassandra problem develops, the sheer increase of available data in support of the mistrusted party's trustworthiness becomes counterproductive. For the problem does not derive from want of evidence, but from an error of judgement. According to O'Neill, to rectify this would require, first, getting clearer about the expectations placed on the potential trustee and, second, agreeing on a clear procedure whereby everyone can see that these expectations are reasonably met.

Clearly, this solution heads in the opposite direction to what is suggested by an affective model of trust. As seen earlier, Thomas (1990) makes a case for an ethical relationship where interpersonal trust flows from the mutual recognition of one another's moral worth. To do so, it consciously departs from the language of rights and obligations. By contrast, intelligent accountability is about specifying mutual expectations in terms of rights and obligations and putting in place formal structures, by dint of which obligation-bearers are held accountable and right-holders prevented from mistrusting them for no good reason (O'Neill 2005).

Miller's proposal contains elements of both models of trust. In itself, this might seem unsurprising. For the proposal is based on the notion of a quasi-contract, and so neither aspires to fully transcend the language of rights and obligations in line with a purely affective approach, nor to comprise all relevant normative requirements in terms of rights and corresponding obligations in line with a purely cognitive approach. Yet, given that these two approaches recommend what seem to be incompatible measures for building and sustaining interpersonal trust, the prospects of bringing them together into a coherent mid-way position look rather dubious. These suspicions are further confirmed if we look at the distribution of affective and cognitive aspects of trust within Miller's proposal. For the general idea that high levels of trust among fellow citizens are required for a successful welfare democracy flows from an affective model. As Jones would have put it, fellow citizens should view one another 'through the affective lens of trust' in order to support redistributive policies across different groups instead of essentially trying to promote their own interests. However, this general model of trust is not extended to immigrant groups: unlike members of the national majority, immigrants are meant to show themselves worthy of trust by integrating into this majority's culture. Again, in itself, this requirement does not seem to be objectionable. The problem arises from the fact that it can be consistently made only within a purely cognitive model of trust. In particular, if the requirement for cultural integration placed on immigrants remains partly unspecified, as suggested by the terms of the quasi-contract favoured by Miller, there will be no way to avoid the Cassandra problem. Neither will receiving nations be sufficiently reassured that immigrants are committed citizens, nor will immigrants be confident of ever being fully accepted. What is more, the very fact that interactions with immigrant groups are conceptualized on a separate model of trust, not the general one covering interactions among fellow citizens, is just as problematic. For instance, Miller argues that immigrants should engage in activities associated with good – as distinct from minimal – citizenship in order to fulfil the quasi-contractual obligation to integrate into the culture of their adopted country (Miller, 2008, p. 381). Yet, no such requirement is explicitly placed on longer-established groups. Their members seem to be either exempt from it or, more likely, assumed to be good citizens by virtue of their – allegedly unproblematic – belonging to the national culture. This co-existence of a general model of trust among citizens, which is implicitly affective, with another model applicable to immigrants, which is primarily cognitive, has even more insidious implications than a Cassandra problem. To see why this is so, let us turn to the second main query identified earlier about interpersonal trust.

Is trust supposed to track or attract trustworthiness?

Drawing on the preceding discussion, it becomes apparent that the affective and cognitive models take opposing views on the relationship between trust and trustworthiness. Conceived as an affective attitude, trust is meant to attract, not to track trustworthiness. For, as we saw earlier, this kind of trust is inseparable from the 'expectation that the one trusted will be directly and favourably moved by the thought that we are counting on her' (Jones 1996, p. 4). In other words, by showing trust, we help motivate trustworthy behaviour. By contrast, conceived as a cognitive attitude, trust is meant to track, not to attract trustworthiness. In fact, this kind of trust is practically indistinguishable from forming only clear and reasonable expectations. Having said that, cognitive trust can also facilitate trustworthy behaviour, albeit indirectly, by removing obstacles, such as misplaced mistrust and other manifestations of the Cassandra problem. Similarly, affective trust is not resistant to evidence to the point of becoming licence to deceive. And so, there seems to be room for coherent hybrid models of trust that build on the strengths of both approaches.[4] Yet, Miller's proposal does not appear to be successful in this respect. Instead, it is likely to lead to what I termed earlier a political circumstance of self-fulfilling distrust. To make clearer the target of this critique, it would be helpful to briefly look at two earlier papers in which Miller succinctly articulates the role of a shared national identity. Consider the following pair of statements:

(1) Deliberation can only succeed where there exists a fairly high level of mutual trust in the deliberating body, which is why I argue that a shared national identity is close to being a necessary prerequisite.
(Miller 2003a, p. 365)

> (2) We may disagree politically with the other side, we may even despise much of what they stand for [...] we know that they still have a good deal in common with us – a language, a history, a cultural background. So we can trust them at least to respect the rules and spirit of democratic government.
>
> (Miller 2003b, p. 117)

What we see here is a one-way relationship of dependence, which runs from common background to mutual trust, to successful democratic interactions. For, as emphasized in (2), disagreement and diversity are potentially problematic and erosive of interpersonal trust. And so, the task of a common background is, as it were, to absorb intractable disagreements, which, in the absence of such background, would presumably result in a loss of mutual trust between citizens who find one another's political views by and large contemptible. But why would a common background in general or a shared national identity in particular, to weave in statement (1), be deemed conducive to mutual trust in the first instance? Looking at statement (2) again, it becomes clear that the knowledge of having a good deal in common is expected to function more like a shield against endemic suspicion rather than to sustain interpersonal trust. On this picture, the idea that a shared national identity seems to provide fellow citizens with the implicit assurance that no one is capable of disappointing the other too much, or in too unpredictable a way. To the extent that this is still a model of interpersonal trust, it would be one where trustworthiness is conceived as, if not replaced by, predictability.

If this conjecture is correct, the problem that Miller's proposal attempts to solve turns out to be misconceived. That is to say, a shared national identity, which is apparently required to boost interpersonal trust weakened by cultural diversity, might in fact be required in order to cover for diminishing trust in the national institutions. Arguably, the very demand for high levels of interpersonal trust could indicate a widespread institutional failure – to provide well-structured cooperative environments where trust across different groups is the norm.[5] To explain this phenomenon, Niklas Luhmann (1988, p. 98) draws a distinction between trust and confidence:

> The normal case is that of confidence. You are confident that your expectations will not be disappointed. [...] Trust, on the other hand, requires a previous engagement on your part. It presupposes a situation of risk. [...] The distinction between confidence and trust thus depends on perception and attribution. If you do not consider the alternatives (every morning you leave the house without a weapon!), you are in a situation of confidence. If you choose one action in preference to others in spite of the possibility of being disappointed by the action of others, you define the situation as one of trust.

On this view, trust is reserved for identifiable parties and relationships, whereas confidence concerns the context in which the parties meet and relationships take place. Luhmann's distinction between trust and confidence has an important implication for the present discussion: the lack of confidence and the resulting demand for trust tend to form a vicious circle whereby trust becomes impossible. To illustrate this point, Luhmann considers a case of a corrupt legal system. Doing business within such a system is incredibly risky. The danger of being cheated is great, for any contractual obligations would be practically unenforceable. And so, lack of confidence in the relevant institutions would be very well-founded. Furthermore, it would make trust among business partners vital. However, it would also make it inadvisable. Given the corrupt institutional framework that allows untrustworthy behaviours to pay off, even in the long run and not only in one-off transactions, why should anyone trust anyone else?[6] When confidence is lacking, no one can afford to trust the others, although they all sincerely share an interest in high levels of interpersonal trust.

Let us look again at Miller's presentation of the problem of trust within a democratic welfare state. If Miller is correct that citizenship alone cannot ground interpersonal trust within such a state, so citizens have to rely on sharing a cultural identity 'of the kind that common nationality provides', the situation described will be relevantly similar to the vicious circle of lacking confidence and needed trust that we just considered. In terms of the preceding discussion, trust would not be able either to track or to attract trustworthiness. Instead, it would be tasked with an impossible mission – to compensate for the lack of propitious institutional settings. For, when such settings are not sufficiently established, interpersonal distrust becomes the default position. What is more, since the focus of political attention shifts away from public institutions to private citizens, this kind of distrust is likely to become self-fulfilling. As Diego Gambetta (1988, p. 234) observes:

> Trust is a peculiar belief predicated not on evidence but on the lack of contrary evidence – a feature that [...] makes it vulnerable to deliberate destruction. In contrast, deep distrust is very difficult to invalidate through experience, for either it prevents people from engaging in the appropriate kind of social experiment, or, worse, it leads to behaviour which bolsters the validity of distrust itself. Once distrust has set in, it soon becomes impossible to know if it has ever in fact been justified, for it has the capacity to be self-fulfilling, to generate a reality consistent with itself. It then becomes individually 'rational' to behave accordingly, even for those previously prepared to act on more optimistic expectations.

To reflect the political origins of the kind of self-fulfilling distrust at issue here – as argued earlier, it derives from considering citizenship insufficient for trust among citizens – it seems apt to term it 'the political circumstance of self-fulfilling distrust'. To the extent that it presents a failure to trust when trust is both appropriate and required, the political circumstance of self-fulfilling distrust is similar to the Cassandra problem. However, in the political case, this failure goes well beyond a cognitive bias, for it has a distinctly prejudicial effect on some potentially marginalized groups of citizens. This is a direct consequence of associating trust among citizens with sharing a national culture as opposed to citizenship. For citizens deemed insufficiently integrated into this culture would be held responsible for a deficit of interpersonal trust that is in fact highly detrimental to them as they are the ones whose trustworthiness would be routinely questioned. What is more, they would have little chance for redress. As it emerged from the preceding discussion, volunteering evidence of trustworthiness, such as successful cultural integration, is unlikely to help. Only trust can attract trustworthiness, not the other way around.

National culture and non-domination

Miller's conception of interpersonal trust based on a shared national culture has attracted wide critical interest. For instance, Matthew Festenstein argues in a recent paper that this conception 'fails to specify how trust in the public sphere is to be generated, in the circumstances of disagreement that give rise to the need for political deliberation and democratic decision in the first place' (Festenstein 2009, p. 292). Nevertheless, Festenstein concedes: 'Sharing an identity may eliminate some sources of distrust – but so may sharing other sorts of non-national identity, such as ethnicity and religion. But this shared identity only serves to create a space within which the politics of trust still has to be negotiated by those concerned' (p. 293).[7]

The conclusion supported by Festenstein's argument is that Miller's conception is ineffective in the promotion of trust. The line of critique pursued here has gone a step further to suggest that this conception creates a political circumstance of self-fulfilling distrust. So far, I have argued for this claim primarily by reflecting on the nature and basis of trust. In the remainder of this paper, I shall briefly remark on the role of national culture in Miller's proposal. This will help bring into relief the distinctly prejudicial effect this proposal could have for potentially marginalized groups of immigrants and citizens alike. The following argument partly draws on the account of epistemic injustice proposed by Miranda Fricker (2007) and more specifically, on the notion of identity-prejudicial credibility deficit. According to Fricker, such credibility deficit arises from the entrenched perception of certain groups as unreliable knowers, e.g. because they are deemed too lazy, or emotional, or stupid. As a result, they are considered as less trustworthy than the average. What is more, their intentions are treated as relatively insignificant. This is because what makes them unworthy of trust is their perceived lack of epistemic competence, not the suspicion that they might use such competence to deceive. The resulting credibility deficit can be seen as identity-prejudicial in two ways. First, it is based on a prejudice that attaches to some group identities, including that of women in sexist cultures and racial minorities in segregated societies. Second, it undermines the standing of those affected within the community of knowers.

A requirement to integrate into a national culture in order to become a trustworthy citizen might lead to a different kind of identity-prejudicial credibility deficit. What I have in mind is an asymmetrical expectation placed on presumed outsiders, but not insiders: to accept a great deal of things about public life on blind trust, without a principled argument.[8] This looks like an inescapable conclusion of the way national culture is conceptualized on Miller's proposal. Sharing a cultural identity 'of the kind that common nationality provides' is presented as a prerequisite for successful democratic deliberation. At the same time, this identity is interpreted as separate from citizenship as shared political membership. So the national culture of a liberal democratic state is not conceived as a particular manifestation of some universal principles of political morality, but as an independent source of political normativity on a par with these principles. As a result, the requirement to partake in some cultural practices would be justifiable on purely conventional grounds, by appeal to the 'done thing' in this country. To appreciate the difference between conventional and principled justification, let us consider a helpful example offered by Nicholas Southwood (2011, p. 778):

> if a Canadian's judgement that one must bring a bottle of wine for one's host when invited for dinner is grounded in part in a social practice of bringing a bottle of wine for one's host when invited for dinner, this means that it somehow appears to the Canadian that the practice among Canadians of bringing a bottle of wine for one's host when invited for dinner is a non-derivative aspect of what justifies the requirement to bring a bottle of wine for one's host when invited for dinner.

This non-derivative aspect of conventional justification might be seen as an advantage worth absorbing into a notion of national culture. For it could seem well-aligned with the idea of liberal neutrality: the social practices immigrants are expected to fit in are not presented as morally superior to the practices they are used to. Neither better, nor worse: just how things are done here. At a close look, however, this conceptualization turns out to be problematic. This is because of the political significance attached to cultural integration on Miller's view: it is a prerequisite for fully partaking in democratic deliberation, not the other way around. If so, perceived outsiders of the national culture cannot escape a lesser, if not entirely passive, role in the democratic process. For on some matters, it would seem appropriate not to convince them by means of a principled argument as it befits fellow citizens, but by appeal to how things are done here. What is more, alleged cultural outsiders who refuse to take such appeals on blind trust might find themselves even further marginalized as unable to integrate into, if not hostile to, the nation's culture.

To see why this is so, let us look again at Southwood's example, the Canadian practice of bringing a bottle of wine for one's host when invited for dinner. Scepticism about this practice would have different consequences for Canadians depending on whether their belonging to the national culture is widely recognized or questioned. The former would be free to express disagreement, if not contempt for the practice: 'Bringing a bottle of wine when invited for dinner – what a silly thing to do! There are much better ways of showing friendliness and appreciation for one's host!' They might be criticized as eccentric, curmudgeonly or stingy. It is unlikely, however, that their national identity as Canadians will ever come into question. In contrast, a similar scepticism expressed by alleged cultural outsiders is likely to be seen not as a view worthy of critical discussion, but as a sign of their ignorance of, or disaffection with, the Canadian ways. By construing national culture in conventional terms, independent of citizenship, we risk ingraining this kind of identity-prejudicial credibility deficit at the level of democratic deliberation.

Acknowledgments

I would like to thank Iseult Honohan and an anonymous reviewer for their helpful comments on an earlier draft of this paper.

Notes

1. This paper focuses on cases where the quasi-contract benefits a receiving nation to the detriment of immigrant groups. Instances of the opposite kind of one-sidedness – quasi-contracts that disadvantage a receiving nation by being too favourable to immigrant groups – will not be given separate consideration: firstly, because these two kinds of possible imbalances raise separate sets of conceptual issues; and secondly, because quasi-contracts favouring immigrants over receiving nations are less likely given the balance of power between the parties involved. On this latter point, see, for instance, Carens (1987).
2. See also Southwood (2011, pp. 765ff.), which drew my attention to the philosophical interest of this passage.
3. John Locke's conception of government as ultimate trustee or deputy of the people is a classic example of institutional as opposed to interpersonal understanding of political trust. See especially §§221–222 and 240 of *The Second Treatise* (1960) where Locke expands on the idea that the people remain the ultimate judge of whether the government has breached their trust and lost its legitimacy as a result. See also Hardin (1999) and Harré (1999), who provide complementary perspectives on the distinction between interpersonal and institutional trust in politics. On the significance of the concept of trust in the history of modern political philosophy, see Gough (1973), esp. ch. 7 'Political Trusteeship'. According to Gough, trust has become a central political concept for it provides, by means of a legal metaphor, a useful vehicle for the idea of an obligation which – although enforceable – is so not as a matter of strict law, but of good conscience. Miller's account of trust as grounded in a quasi-contract stands in direct continuity with this tradition.
4. Examples include Hardin (1991) and Pettit (1995). Hardin's account has the merit of demonstrating how some refusals to trust – although justified in cognitive terms, e.g. when the potential cost of misplacing trust is relatively high – are not fully rational, for they prevent the distrustful person from engaging in potentially trusting relationships. Pettit's account elucidates the effectiveness of openly placing one's trust in others, e.g. 'I count on you!', and explains this phenomenon as 'the cunning of trust', based partly on evidence and prediction, partly on our sense of common humanity.

5. See, for instance, Offe (1999), according to whom trust among fellow citizens is supported by trust in the democratic institutions, not the other way around. The subsequent discussion draws on this account, especially on the contrast between democratic institutions and national identity as alternative foundations of trust among citizens.
6. Cf. Williams (1995), p. 116: 'Co-operation requires trust in the sense that dependent parties need some degree of assurance that non-dependent parties will not defect, [...] in general, people will not trust others enough to bring about co-operation unless their assurance is to some extent well based: that is to say, unless in fact people are generally motivated, one way or another, not to defect if they are in a non-dependent position.'
7. Abizadeh (2002) is another critical response to Miller, which helped shape the current analysis. See also McBride (2010), who raises a related challenge to Miller's proposal: in the context of a multinational state, cultivating distinct national identities is unlikely to warrant greater civic trust. This conclusion is consistent with the argument advanced here; however, it is reached from a premise that is not shared by the current analysis. According to this premise, trust is not necessary for a well-functioning democracy.
8. Drawing on Pettit (2001), ch. 5, I assume that the credibility deficit at issue is inconsistent with freedom as non-domination. This is because, in Pettit's terms, cultural outsiders, be they citizens or not, would lack the discursive control to counter arbitrary intrusions from insiders. Pettit describes a situation of shared discursive control as follows: 'When we discourse, or reason together, about a theoretical or practical problem we recognise it as a common problem. [...] Recognising it as a common problem, then, we search for considerations that we can recognise in common as relevant to its resolution, and we look for a resolution that we can agree in common is supported by those considerations' (p. 67). Those who suffer from the kind of identity-prejudicial credibility deficit identified here are dominated by virtue of being excluded from the 'we' of shared discursive control.

Notes on contributor

Lubomira Radoilska is an Affiliated Lecturer at the Faculty of Philosophy, University of Cambridge. She is author of *Aristotle and the moral philosophy of today* (Presses Universitaires de France 2007) and *Addiction and weakness of will* (Oxford University Press 2013), and editor of *Autonomy and mental disorder* (Oxford University Press 2012).

References

Abizadeh, A., 2002. Does liberal democracy presuppose a cultural nation? Four arguments. *American political science review*, 96, 495–509.

Baier, A., 1986. Trust and antitrust. *Ethics*, 96, 231–260.

Carens, J., 1987. Aliens and citizens: the case for open borders. *The review of politics*, 49 (2), 251–273.

Cole, P., 2010. Introduction: 'border crossings' – the dimensions of membership. *In*: G. Calder, P. Cole and J. Seglow, eds. *Citizenship acquisition and national belonging: migration, membership and the liberal democratic state*. Palgrave Macmillan: Basingstoke, 1–23.

Festenstein, M., 2009. National identity, political trust and the public realm. *Critical review of international social and political philosophy*, 12 (2), 279–296.

Forster, E.M., 1924. *A Passage to India*. New York: Harcourt, Brace and Company.

Fricker, M., 2007. *Epistemic injustice: power and the ethics of knowing*. Oxford: Oxford University Press.

Gambetta, D., 1988. Can we trust trust? *In*: D. Gambetta, ed. *Trust: Making and breaking cooperative relations*. Oxford: Blackwell, 213–237.

Gough, J.W., 1973. *John Locke's political philosophy*. 2nd ed. Oxford: Oxford University Press.

Hardin, R., 1991. The street-level epistemology of trust. *Politics and society*, 21, 505–529.

Hardin, R., 1999. Do we want trust in government? *In*: M. Warren, ed. *Democracy and trust*. Cambridge: Cambridge University Press, 22–41.

Harré, R., 1999. Trust and its surrogates: psychological foundations of the political process. *In*: M. Warren, ed. *Democracy and trust*. Cambridge: Cambridge University Press, 249–272.

Holton, R., 1994. Deciding to trust, coming to believe. *Australasian journal of philosophy*, 72, 63–76.

Jones, K., 1996. Trust as an affective attitude. *Ethics*, 107, 4–25.

Locke, J., 1960. *Two treatises of government*. Cambridge: Cambridge University Press.

Luhmann, N., 1988. Familiarity, confidence, trust: problems and alternatives. *In*: D. Gambetta, ed. *Trust: making and breaking cooperative relations*. Oxford: Blackwell.

McBride, C., 2010. Postnationalist democratization: rethinking nationality, trust, and accountability. *In*: K. Breen and S. O'Neill. eds. *After the nation?* Basingstoke: Palgrave, 161–176.

Miller, D., 1995. *On nationality*. Oxford: Clarendon Press.

Miller, D., 2000. *Citizenship and national identity*. Cambridge: Polity Press.

Miller, D., 2003a. A response. *In*: D.A. Bell and A. De-Shalit, eds. *Forms of justice: critical perspectives on David Miller's political philosophy*. Lanham, MD: Rowman and Littlefield, 349–372.

Miller, D., 2003b. *Political philosophy: a very short introduction*. Oxford: Oxford University Press.

Miller, D., 2008. Immigrants, nations, and citizenship. *Journal of political philosophy*, 16, 371–390.

O'Neill, O., 2002a. *A question of trust*. Cambridge: Cambridge University Press.

O'Neill, O., 2002b. *Autonomy and trust in bioethics*. Cambridge: Cambridge University Press.

O'Neill, O., 2005. *Justice, trust and accountability*. Transcript of lecture, dated 18 March 2005. *Cambridge*: Casimir Lewy Library Offprint Collection.

Offe, C., 1999. How can we trust our fellow citizens? *In*: M. Warren, ed. *Democracy and trust*. Cambridge: Cambridge University Press, 42–87.

Pettit, P., 1995. The cunning of trust. *Philosophy and public affairs*, 24, 202–225.

Pettit, P., 2001. *A theory of freedom. From the psychology to the politics of agency*. Cambridge: Polity Press.

Southwood, N., 2011. The moral/convention distinction. *Mind*, 120 (479), 761–802.

Thomas, L., 1990. Trust, affirmation, and moral character: A critique of Kantian morality. *In*: O. Flanagan and A.O. Rorty, eds. *Identity, character, and morality*. Cambridge, MA: MIT Press, 235–257.

Williams, B., 1995. Formal structures and social reality. *In*: B. Williams, *Making sense of humanity*. Cambridge: Cambridge University Press, 111–122.

Competing methods of territorial control, migration and justice

Christopher Bertram

Philosophy, University of Bristol, Bristol, UK

Many accounts of justice and migration focus on the spatial exclusion of migrants. This article argues that two modes of exclusion, one spatial and the other social, are of normative interest. It explores the merits and demerits of territorial and social boundary exclusion from the point of view of justice. Territorial exclusion offends against freedoms of movement and association; social boundary exclusion undermines status equality among those subject to the same laws. Explicit awareness that modern states use both modes of exclusion is a prerequisite for clear thinking about migration justice.

Introduction

This paper argues that a distinction taken from the literature of social anthropology between 'perimeter defence' and 'social boundary defence' can be illuminating in helping us to think about issues of territory and migration. First, it can help us go beyond legalistic and state-centric categories to look at real behaviours and outcomes. Second, it can cause us to look again at the moral acceptability of border controls and immigration restrictions. It argues that social boundary defence – restricting access to membership rather than territory – seems to offer an alternative to border control that could reconcile the cosmopolitan commitment to freedom of movement with the putatively legitimate claims of national groups. However, this is somewhat illusory, as it would lead to the unacceptable situation that persons might become long-term residents on a state's territory without similar rights and opportunities to other residents. Such an outcome fails to meet reasonable standards of democratic legitimacy and reciprocity, and exposes non-citizens on the territory to exploitation.

State, territory, membership

The modern state is a legal and political entity that is essentially territorial in nature. States exercise sovereignty over a given territory, and this takes the form of claiming the authority to exercise jurisdiction over those who live within its borders, specifying the systems of property and justice they are subject to, and threatening or exercising coercive force in support of those systems. Within their territory, states also do many other things, such as providing external defence, welfare systems, physical infrastructure, and so on. Since the jurisdiction states exercise is territorially based, states also claim the right to control their borders and to determine who or what may cross them.[1] The problem of immigration, seen in the light of this conception of the modern state, appears first as a problem of space and jurisdiction: there is a legal authority with respect to a territory and the issue is one of whether to permit a person to cross physically into that area or whether to stop them from doing so.

It seems natural for us to think in these terms regarding states and migration. Even when we challenge the claims states make for themselves, the optic within which we make the challenge will often be this spatial and juridical one. So, for example, we might focus on the sheer arbitrariness of borders and on the peculiarity of the notion that states have the right to prevent natural persons from crossing an arbitrary line. Thinking of the issues in this way seems inescapable. Yet we also engage in a related set of arguments concerning migration that, though juridically focused, lack this essentially spatial dimension, but are instead directed towards membership of the society in question. The contrast between the territorial–jurisdictional and the membership angles highlights an uncomfortable aspect of the debate: on the one hand, the subjects of discussion are these legal–territorial entities called states; on the other, they are social groups whose identity can hover uneasily between the set of possessors of citizenship rights and some culturally or ethnically defined group that overlaps only loosely with those who hold citizenship.

Political philosophy, because of its close connection to the philosophy of law and because of the importance many of its leading practitioners have placed on the legally defined basic institutions of society, tends to look at issues of cooperation and justice through a somewhat legalistic lens. An example of this is Rawls (1999b), with his focus on the basic structure. But, as critics of liberalism from Karl Marx to G. A. Cohen have been keen to emphasize, the juridical facts can mislead us about what is really happening, about the real patterns of advantage and disadvantage that exist within and between societies.[2] Literature from other disciplines, such as social anthropology and sociology can help us to uncover these underlying patterns and save us from the temptation to take society's legal self-image at face value.

A distinction from social anthropology

Social anthropologists looking at foraging groups have distinguished between two different strategies of territorial control, both of which aim to preserve a group's control of and access to resources. The first of these looks very much like the border-control strategy employed by states. This 'perimeter defence' strategy involves a group overtly marking a physical boundary and taking steps to control the crossing of that boundary by outsiders. Such crossings are comparatively rare, and, where they occur, usually take place with the permission of the group into whose territory the outsider is crossing. The second, alternative, strategy is 'social boundary defence' and is typically employed by foraging groups when the territory they inhabit is very large and when the resources within it are scarce and thinly dispersed. Social boundary defence abandons the attempt to control a frontier. This is because such perimeter defence can involve a high opportunity cost for the 'insider' group, tying up valuable resources in guarding a line that could otherwise be put to profitable use in hunting and gathering. Instead, groups who employ the social boundary defence restrict access to the social resources they possess, resources that are essential to the efficient exploitation of the environment. In the Australian outback, for example, a group may safely allow outsiders passage across their territory, because without the knowledge of water sources and edible species that only the group knows, outsiders cannot make much use of the space. A group using the social boundary defence may share information with outsiders as and when it is mutually advantageous to do so. It may also permit other groups to stay on the territory when they perform some specific function, perhaps trade or manufacture, that is useful to the dominant group. Groups can therefore remain distinct entities, but overlap in their spatial locations. The key conceptual distinction is set out by Cashdan (1983, pp. 49–50).

When I encountered this distinction, it struck me, first, that it could also be useful in thinking about modern societies and states, their attempts to control access to their territory, and their relationship to immigrants and would-be immigrants who seek to settle and work within their boundaries, and, second, that using one method or the other (or some mix of the two) might be morally preferable. Much discussion of immigration and justice is centred around the rather obvious phenomenon of 'perimeter defence'. States have frontiers and they guard them. They establish checkpoints at ports and airports, they patrol the seas, they try to establish physical barriers such as the one on the US–Mexican border to prevent crossings, or the razor wire surrounding the Spanish enclaves in North Africa. Multi-state groupings such as the European Union develop specialized agencies such as Frontex to prevent would be migrants from crossing the Mediterranean into Europe's southern border. At the time of writing, most European citizens seem totally unaware even of the existence of Frontex (Neal 2009).

But preventing frontier crossing is, in fact, just one of the strategies that states and societies employ towards outsiders. States also use various means to restrict the extent to which those foreigners who are present within the territory can become a part of the functioning society on similar terms to full citizens. These means may include juridical means, such as restrictions on access to citizenship or permanent residence, restriction of other political rights, restrictions on freedom to participate in the labour market via work permits and other restrictions. But to these formal legal barriers of various kinds we can add the informal obstacles that outsiders face and the extent to which the state enables or impedes outsiders in their attempts to overcome them. Is the state prepared to challenge racial or religious intolerance among the majority population? Are there difficult language obstacles to labour market participation by non-nationals? An outsider group may not face explicit legal obstacles to labour-market participation, but it may be that its members only get access to certain trades or activities and have little chance of securing more prestigious forms of employment.

In controlling access to their territory, states never employ pure versions of either perimeter defence or social boundary defence, but rather some combination of the two. They both police their boundaries by trying to control who may and who may not enter their jurisdiction, and they also regulate the extent to which outsiders can and do penetrate the social body. When we look at issues of territorial justice in the light of the distinction between the two ideal types of territorial control, we may come to see state policies and strategies that look very different to one another, because of the way in which they either prevent or permit the physical presence of outsiders within the jurisdiction, as being simply different ways of achieving the same objective.

Exclusionary strategies and justice

Our interest in migration and migration rights from within political philosophy is twofold. First, there is the question of whether the goal of maintaining the boundaries of a state or a 'people' in Rawls's (1999a, §2) sense is legitimate at all. Do states have the right to exclude outsiders? Conversely, do outsiders have rights not to be excluded? In this discussion, I largely leave this fundamental question to one side, in order to look at the legitimacy and justice of the two methods we might use to maintain the boundary. Is one or the other better or worse from the point of view of justice?

In discussing the relative merits of the two exclusionary strategies, we need to keep in mind two sets of values, both of which plausibly answer to some of the demands of justice. On the one side are a set of goals that we can call, as a shorthand, 'nationalist'. With this term, I intend to denote a number of goals: the legitimate interest of a people in maintaining its collective autonomy, in being a self-determining entity, and in exercising any collective right to freedom of association it might have (Wellman 2008); the collective interest a people has in providing welfare and health services for its members on fair and sustainable terms; a similar collective interest in providing public goods at a desirable level and in preventing free-riding; their collective interest in regulating labour markets, including for the benefit of their least advantaged citizens, and so on. If there is a legitimate national interest in such matters as the preservation of language and culture, then we can also add these to the list. On the other side are goals and goods that have no such special connection to particular societies, but are attached to human beings as such wherever they are. Again, we can call these goods, for shorthand, 'cosmopolitan goods'. These include the interests that human beings have in individual freedom of association, in freedom of movement (Carens 1987), in personal security, in opportunities for economic enhancement and in the furtherance and protection of a range of capabilities, functionings and in the protection of basic human rights. Universalist principles of justice, such as luck egalitarianism (Cohen 1989), and universalist consequentialisms, such as utilitarianism and prioritarianism (Parfit 2000), are also species of cosmopolitan value.

These nationalist or cosmopolitan values can feature in our argument in three ways. First, if an exclusionary strategy has the property of better promoting some of these goals than the alternative would, then that provides a pro tanto reason in favour of that strategy. Second, a value can be of such importance that it simply rules a strategy or a particular version of a strategy out of consideration. So, for example, the fact that an exclusionary strategy is incompatible with a basic human right provides a compelling reason to reject it in all but the most extreme and unusual circumstances (and perhaps even then). Third, such goals will often feature in an argument that purports to justify some policy on the grounds that the policy is necessary to the achievement of the goal. Consideration of some version of an alternative exclusionary strategy can undermine such arguments by demonstrating that it is in fact false that the goal can only be pursued in that manner. Given the messy nature of the real world, however, we are unlikely to find arguments that count conclusively and decisively in favour of one strategy and against the other. More likely, we will see that the balance of reasons somewhat favours one rather than the other, or suggests some mix of strategies.

The perimeter-defence strategy

How then does the perimeter-defence strategy fare in relation to these nationalist and cosmopolitan goals? Arguments are often advanced that perimeter defence is justified because of legitimate nationalist goals. On the other hand, most of the literature that is hostile to border controls emphasizes their negative impact on cosmopolitan values.

Considering first the cosmopolitan values, it is easy to see the basic elements of the cosmopolitan case against border controls. First, border controls are coercive, and, as such, they interfere with the freedom of would-be migrants.[3] Second, if people have a specific right to freedom of movement then border controls violate that right. Third, border controls interfere with individual freedom of association in various ways: economically, their freedom to contract with others in employment or for the provision of goods and services is restricted; more personally, border controls inhibit their ability to form and pursue friendships, family and romantic associations with others.[4] Fourth, border controls seem inconsistent with some widely held intuitions about justice because they prevent people from moving from a less to a more economically developed jurisdiction. If it is unjust for people to be worse off than others through no fault of their own, then a system that confines individual opportunity to a poorer jurisdiction just because of accident of birth and nationality also looks to be unjust. Finally, we can adduce general consequentialist reasons against border controls: on a standard utilitarian view, border controls are bad because they artificially block the efficient allocation of labour as resource; on some prioritarian version of consequentialism they are also bad because they impose a lower standard of living on the already-disadvantaged than would be the case under some alternative, open borders regime.

From a nationalist point of view, on the other hand, perimeter defence can look more promising. It enables governments to keep track of who is and who is not located on the national territory, and so is arguably an efficient and convenient tool that can assist a people in pursuing its legitimate collective goals. Such goals as collective freedom of association, economic and demographic policy, environmental and cultural preservation, and so forth, are much easier to pursue if governments are in a position to control who is, and who is not, in the country. On the other hand, arguments of necessity seem overstated. In order to exercise its collective rights of self-determination and freedom of association or to maintain its cultural integrity, a people does not normally physically need to keep outsiders out of its physical space. In order to exercise its collective democratic rights of self-determination, a people does not need physically to exclude outsiders, since the relevant variable is not their physical location but their citizenship status: citizens participate in elections etc. and tourists, Gastarbeiter, etc. do not. Most foreigners are denied the right to vote and some foreigners (such as most European Union citizens in the UK) are granted only restricted political rights. Similarly, and contra Christopher Heath Wellman (2008), collective freedom of association does not normally require spatial exclusion since, whether a group of persons associates with other groups or individuals is not a matter of spatial location but of behaviour. One case for freedom of association is labour-market participation. Most foreigners require work permits in order to work legally. A further area relevant to freedom of association is where outsiders are denied full rights in relation to property ownership, where historically and actually, many jurisdictions restrict the rights of foreigners. No doubt these examples could be multiplied. The case of cultural identity, for want of a better term, is rather similar. First, it is unlikely that large numbers would choose to move to an area if they were denied access to the social infrastructure of the dominant group (and, to the extent that they are, the 'problem' may disappear in another way, through their absorption into the dominant group[5]). But, in any case, cultural identity is also not primarily a matter of spatial location and fences and perimeters are not necessary to maintain it, as has been shown in the case of diaspora groups who successfully control their own boundaries and membership despite not having territorial jurisdiction or the power to keep outsiders out of their physical neighbourhood. If subaltern groups can maintain their distinctness without such measures, it ought to be all the easier for groups that are locally dominant and control the state apparatus to do so.

We can also cast doubt on similar claims made concerning the incompatibility of the right to freedom of movement with the existence of welfare states and the supply of public goods at a desirable level (Perry 1995, Heath 1997). These claims are clearly incorrect, since it would be perfectly possible for a state to permit migrants and other foreigners to enter its territory in a manner consistent with a right to free movement, but also to deny them access to a range of possible goods and services. In fact, to some extent this already happens. With respect to state-funded health and welfare systems, access rights are often dependent on citizenship or contribution, and aliens often fail to meet the criteria. Some public goods having to do with the physical infrastructure of the country are such that it would be impossible to exclude aliens from their consumption, but it does not seem likely that this would be a problem so grave as to undermine the tax base that pays for them. Insofar as we believe that control of valuable natural resources should rest with the people who inhabit a territory, this does not require perimeter defence either. Valuable mineral resources or airspace could be under the direct control of the state in question. Alternatively, the property regime could be so organized as to deny aliens on the territory the right to control resources.

Additionally, we can note that the perimeter-defence strategy introduces all kinds of inefficiencies. To give one example, the perimeter strategy is the way in which it disrupts traditional patterns of seasonal migration and effectively forces people into once and forever choices about where they are to live. For example, before the US–Mexican border became so tightly controlled, many Mexicans would travel to California to earn money, picking fruit for American farmers before returning to their home villages after the harvest. The option to go and return in this way is effectively closed now, and Mexicans who want to go to work in the United States must choose to travel one way, or, if they return, must face the difficult and potentially lethal journey back to the United States again. Understandably, far fewer are willing to do this than were willing to migrate seasonally in the past.

To sum up then, on the perimeter-defence strategy: it is generally very negative with respect to the cosmopolitan goods whilst not being strictly necessary for the defence of the nationalist ones. This might give us hope that the putative alternative, the social boundary strategy, would be more acceptable from the point of view of justice, perhaps finding a way of promoting the nationalist values in a way compatible with also respecting the cosmopolitan ones.

The social boundary strategy

The social boundary strategy, to repeat, involves controlling the social boundary of a group rather than using spatial exclusion. It permits non-members to be physically present on the territory but denies then access to many of the goods available to group members, at the discretion of the dominant group. Whilst it may not be practical or feasible to exclude outsiders from the full range of goods on the territory – beautiful vistas, a cooling summer breeze – many goods, such as access to health care and welfare systems or to labour markets can be denied to them, or provided on a selective and different basis to those provided to outsiders. This degree of social exclusion is the normal status of many foreigners today, tourists for example. If I travel to, say, the United States as a tourist, my right to be physically present on the territory of the United States does not give me access to many of the services and opportunities available to US citizens and permanent residents: I have no entitlement to US social security, nor do I have the right to seek and take employment in the United States, as the labour market is closed to me. A generalized version of this strategy would, then, allow open borders but restrict social participation.

With respect to some of the cosmopolitan values, principally those to do with freedom of various kinds, this would be an improvement over the perimeter-defence strategy. If freedom of movement is a basic right, then its denial is an injustice, and an exclusionary strategy that does not restrict it is to be preferred. Now there are obvious problems here with any claim that freedom of movement is a basic right that defeats any attempt by states to restrict movement across borders. It isn't clear, for instance, what interests could ground a right to freedom of movement as extensive as this, nor is it clear why other, apparently acceptable, restrictions on freedom of movement within the borders of states placed by such institutions as private property are not equally offensive to the putative basic right (Miller 2007, pp. 201–213). No matter, even if extensive freedom of movement is not a basic right that would ground something like an open borders principle, it is arguably a significant good to have such freedom of movement, both in itself and in virtue of the many opportunities it offers to individuals, some of them economic, but also in respect of other interests in association and just in seeing more of the world. Given this, it is clearly an advantage to an exclusionary strategy that it permits individuals to continue to enjoy the good of freedom of movement whilst simultaneously protecting or promoting legitimate nationalist goals.

Similarly, since the enforcement of border controls requires some directly coercive measures against would-be immigrants, it is, other things being equal, better if such coercion can be avoided. Looked at in a framework of negative and positive duties, we might also think of the social boundary defence as superior. After all, it involves refraining from activities restricting the freedom of intending immigrants and acting directly in ways that are harmful to them, whilst merely refusing to do what we arguably have no strict obligation to do, namely proffering assistance.

Is the social boundary strategy, then, an acceptable alternative from the point of view of justice or for any other reason? Unfortunately not. If the perimeter-defence strategy looks bad, the social boundary strategy may even be worse as regards justice.[6] This is because it allows the medium to long-term presence on the territory of the state of people with lesser rights and opportunities than those possessed by regular members of society. It isn't at all hard to point to some pretty nasty historical and contemporary examples of this. The restriction of European Jews to certain trades and to living in ghettos, apartheid in South Africa, some features of the Israel–Palestine situation, or the presence in Germany of the ethnically Turkish children of Gastarbeiter, denied citizenship because of the essentially hereditary German citizenship rule. One could add to this list the very large numbers of illegal and undocumented migrants in wealthy countries, at least for those cases where their presence is something tacitly condoned by the state authorities: formally, they ought to have been kept out at the perimeter, but actually they are necessary to the well-functioning of the economy. A variant of the social boundary defence is currently finding favour with the British coalition government, who propose to restrict the right of permanent settlement in the UK to small group of wealthy people whilst restricting nearly all other non-European Union foreign workers to temporary status (Cavanagh 2011), measures supplemented in the 2013 Queen's Speech with further restrictions on migrants' access to health and welfare services. In a recent interview, former coalition minister Sarah Teather revealed that the internal ministerial group charged with making UK policy in the area was originally called the 'hostile environment' group (*The Guardian*, 12 July 2013).

There are multiple reasons why the long-term presence of such second-class residents and workers who are excluded from membership is offensive to justice. I shall mention three here: democratic legitimacy; reciprocity and exploitation.

Democratic legitimacy and political exclusion

First, there is the thought that they are subject to the same laws as everybody else, so should have some part in making them at least if present on the territory for some suitably extended period of time. Political power is one of the resources that are available to people within society, and questions arise as to its proper distribution. Many people believe that the correct answer to this question of the distribution of political power is in some sense an egalitarian one (Christiano 1996). On this view, the long term of permanent exclusion from political decision-making of those subject to the law breaches a principle of democratic legitimacy. (Of course this principle presupposes some further claim that people have a right to a democratic say, a claim that has not gone uncontested in recent political philosophy.)

Equality and reciprocity

Second, there are issues to do with equality and reciprocity: if resident foreign workers make a contribution to society on similar terms to its regular members, by, for example, paying taxes that finance benefits, they should be permitted to gain an equality of status.[7] One of the features that the social boundary defence attempts to impose on non-citizens within a society is to limit the range of cooperative activities they engage in. People come to a country to plug a particular gap in the labour market, perhaps to do some particular job. Not allowing them full participation in society is a bit like treating them as external contractor with whom we make a specific deal because it is mutually advantageous to do so. But thinking about the individuals concerned as external contractors seems multiply misguided. People who are resident in a country for a longish period of time put down roots, make friends, perhaps have children. So to think of them via just one of their connections to the wider society mis-describes the human and social reality. Any attempt to enforce a one-dimensional connection to the wider society, by denying such people the right to bring their families with them, perhaps forcing them to live in hostels, etc. would be yet worse, since this would be to deny some of their most basic human rights and needs.

Exploitation and vulnerability

Third, for many of the cases I mentioned there are issues to do with exploitation. Albert Hirschman famously argued that participants in social institutions have a choice between three strategies: exit, voice and loyalty (Hirschman 1970). But second-class residents may well be denied, because of the way in which the social boundary functions, access to alternative ways of making a living and leaving the country may not be an option, they may be denied a voice because of their lack of political rights and ineligibility to join trade unions and other organizations. Faced with the absence of exit or voice as viable strategies, they may be left with putting up with exploitative conditions uncomplainingly. Whilst a lack of options makes people vulnerable, so does their lack of representation within the political system. As Amartya Sen has shown, the fact that politicians do not need to take account of the interests of this or that group exposes them to risk of serious harms in cases of natural disaster or famine: they will be placed last in the queue (Sen 1999).

The nature of the social body

A final thought on the social boundary defence as a means of exclusion from the territorial state: modern nation-states, perhaps especially democratic ones, have a somewhat schizophrenic character when it comes to their identity. On the one hand, they are simply the Weberian entities that exercise the monopoly of legitimate violence over a given territory; on the other hand, they represent 'peoples' with a somewhat indeterminate history and cultural character. When we think about the right of a people to exercise self-government, there often seems to be a tension between a democratic principle, according to which the demos should rule and some nationalistic principle, where the subject of government is the ethnos, to use Michael Mann's terms (Mann 2005, ch. 3). When the standard means of territorial exclusion is perimeter defence, even where the political motivation may be somewhat xenophobic, it is possible to draw a fairly sharp line between the non-citizens who are physically excluded and those who live within the territory. Social boundary defence may take forms that cut cleanly between citizens and non-citizens, perhaps cases involving access to health and welfare benefits would be like that, but it looks more susceptible to pernicious ethnic or racial manipulation in ways that exclude or marginalize all people belonging to minority groups. The recent changes to the immigration laws in the US states of Arizona, Louisiana and Alabama are interesting cases in this respect. They purport to be about perimeter defence, but in granting police sweeping powers to detain those they suspect, and in practically obliging those who look 'Mexican' to carry documents proving their immigration status both to avoid arrest and to access basic services such as public schooling, it also establishes or reinforces a social boundary at a different point between those who are and are not properly a part of the social body.

Non-territorial elites and the social boundary defence

Seeing perimeter defence and social boundary defence as just different strategies aimed at the same goal may also make it possible to see the emergence of new exclusionary communities that are invisible if our focus remains limited to states, overt boundaries and physical territory. Social boundary defence is essentially about a group restricting the access of outsiders to certain benefits and about defining a pool for mutually advantageous interaction among individuals whist limiting dealings with outsiders to a 'need to trade' basis, a theme explored by Robert E. Goodin (1981). The nation-state provides one model for this, a model that features quite prominently in the thinking of many anti-cosmopolitan political philosophers of a roughly post-Rawlsian description (Blake 2002, Nagel 2005). Those political philosophers see the community established by the nation-state as being the site of many-sided interactions among co-citizens who owe one another strong duties of distributive justice.

Ties to outsiders are much weaker and established on the basis of mutually advantageous trading, which carries with it no strong obligations of distributive justice but merely, at best, minimal duties of humanitarian assistance. So, on this model, co-citizens of the UK may have fairly egalitarian duties to one another, but no such duties towards the call-centre staff in Bangalore who their companies contract to handle 'customer service' and with whom they may interact on a fairly regular basis.

The political communities of traditional nation-states are not, for most people, communities of choice. So, unless you are someone like Rupert Murdoch, you probably have no discretion to decide which nation-state to belong to.[8] People can and do change their memberships, but they are the exceptions. One conventional nation-state may be an oasis of privilege compared with another one, and may give those born within it much better life chances, but within its boundaries it will certainly contain a mixture of people, some of whom will be healthy, dynamic and productive, and others of whom will be unproductive, unhealthy, vulnerable and, consequently, poor. A nation-state, therefore, both reinforces inter-societal inequalities and, at the same time, mitigates those that occur within its perimeter, especially if it provides health, education and welfare benefits on a need basis funded from general taxation.

But we live in a world where the resources that are valuable to people are increasingly intangible, because they consist of knowledge, expertise and social networks rather than physical stuff, and where those same networks have a more and more globalized character. This raises the possibility that transnational zones of cooperation and reciprocity will emerge among elites who are able to pool the risks and benefits of cooperation among themselves and then deal with those outside of their new community on a strictly contractual case-by-case basis. Clearly, such a cosmopolitan community cannot police its boundaries by a perimeter-defence strategy, because, by its very nature, it straddles and crosses at will conventional frontiers. But what it can do is use something like the social boundary defence to restrict access to the resources that it controls. These reflections are fairly speculative and I do not mean to suggest that virtual communities of privilege based on social boundary defence will supplant those based on citizenship, territory and predominantly perimeter defence any time soon. The premium attracted by mere citizenship in the wealthiest countries is still enormous, and remains the most important dimension of global inequality (Shachar 2009). But we should nevertheless remain aware that the boundaries and frontiers that shape patterns of advantage and disadvantage, and are hence relevant for social justice, are only partly traced by internal and external legal configurations of nation-states.

Conclusions

This paper does not aim to provide anything like a final verdict on the relative justice or injustice of these two methods of territorial control, though, in my view, both result in significant injustice to the excluded. Rather, my aim here is more modest: to put some of the issues on the table and suggest that viewing the debate on territorial rights and migration primarily within the frame set by perimeter defence may distort our understanding of the issues. This distortion can happen in a number of ways. First, and most obviously, it can lead us to argue falsely that certain strategies and policies are necessary for the securing of certain goods when that is not true because of the existence of alternative strategies that would do the same job. The existence of alternative strategies ought, instead, to provoke a discussion about their relative costs and benefits. Perimeter defence looks more acceptable for the fair treatment of all who live and work within a boundary, but it comes at the cost of the denial of rights of free movement and association to individuals. Social boundary defence allows us to preserve those rights of free movement and association, but it comes at the cost of seeming to treat persons who cooperate closely together and are subject to the same law unfairly compared with one another. Though I have argued that perimeter defence might be less offensive to justice than social boundary defence because of the way the latter involves failures of democratic legitimacy, reciprocity and the risk of exploitation, it has to be admitted that the employment of perimeter defence enables citizens of wealthy countries to insulate themselves from some of the more unpleasant facts about the modern world. To the extent to which the global poor are present in the wealthiest countries in the slums of cities or working as agricultural labourers on our farms, the inequality of global order is more present to us than if such people are prevented from immigrating. If production is outsourced to sweatshops in India or Vietnam, the producers of the goods we consume are invisible to us. With the social boundary defence, on the other hand, we see our fellow humans, commissioned to work for us on the basis of mutual self-interest alone, and denied equal status and full political representation. Perimeter defence may therefore be more acceptable to citizens of wealthy democracies as much for its cosmetic advantages as anything.

Finally, the consideration of these alternatives forces us to think about matters of inclusion and exclusion in a more sociological light. If we are focused on perimeter defence then we are, I think, more likely to think in terms of formal rights of citizenship, jurisdiction, sovereignty and other legal–political categories. Since social boundary defence functions with a broader range of techniques, both formal and informal, we are likely to see pattern of advantage and disadvantage that might otherwise be invisible to us and to see greater similarities between the forms of exclusion practised by peoples and those practised by other social groups, including transnational ones.

Acknowledgements

I should like to thank the participants in workshops held in both Newport and Oslo, including Kim Angell, Chris Armstrong, Meghan Benton, Gideon Calder, Jules

Holroyd, Iseult Honohan, Marit Hovdal-Moan, Sune Laegaard, Cara Nine, Jorgen Odalen, David Owen, Jouni Reinikainen, Enzo Rossi, Jonathan Seglow, Christopher Heath Wellman and Stuart White for their comments in discussion.

Notes

1. Though they may recognize an obligation to allow some outsiders to cross the border and enter their territory, as in, for example, the case of refugees, states conceive of such exceptions as voluntary undertakings that can, in principle, be revoked.
2. Think of Cohen's emphasis on the way that ethos is also determinant of the degree of inequality in a society in his Cohen (2008).
3. On the coercive nature of border controls, see Abizadeh (2008, 2010).
4. On individual freedom of association and border controls, see Steiner (2001).
5. In this respect, think of the numbers of British people with Irish or Polish surnames, or French people with Portuguese names, or northern Italians with Slavic names, etc.
6. Note that a policy could be worse from the perspective of justice, whilst being preferable from the point of view of individual migrants. So, for example, a policy might result in more exploitation, whilst providing the exploited with higher income levels than they could otherwise earn. This obviously raises questions that are beyond the scope of the current paper.
7. In the course of an interesting interview, where he is asked about the possibility of combining open borders with the kind of two-tier status involved in the social boundary strategy, Milton Friedman has this to say: 'If you could do that, that would be fine. But I don't believe you can do that. It's not only that it is not politically feasible, I don't think that it is desirable to have two classes of citizens in a society. We want a free society. We want a society in which every individual is treated as an end in themselves. We don't want a society in which some people are in there under blue conditions, others are in there under red conditions, others are in there under black conditions. We want a free society' (http://econlog.econlib.org/archives/2008/06/milton_friedman_10.html).
8. In a step towards the construction of a transnational elite, wealthy states are increasingly drawn to arrangements where they grant residence or citizenship to those who are willing to deposit large amounts of cash in the jurisdiction. For the UK in this respect, see Cavanagh (2011).

Notes on contributor

Christopher Bertram is Professor in Social and Political Philosophy at the University of Bristol. He is author of *Rousseau and the social contract* (Routledge, 2004) and a number of papers in contemporary philosophy and the history of political thought.

References

Abizadeh, A., 2008. Democratic theory and border coercion. *Political theory*, 36 (1), 37.

Abizadeh, A., 2010. Democratic legitimacy and state coercion: A reply to David Miller. *Political theory*, 38 (1), 121–130.

Blake, M., 2002. Distributive justice, state coercion, and autonomy. *Philosophy and public affairs*, 30 (2), 257–296.

Carens, J.H., 1987. Aliens and citizens: the case for open borders. *The review of politics*, 49 (02), 251–273.

Cavanagh, M., 2011. *Guest workers: settlement, temporary economic migration and a critique of the government's plans*. London: Institute for Public Policy Research.

Cashdan., 1983. Territoriality among human foragers: ecological models and an application to four bushman groups. *Current anthropology*, 24 (1), 47–66.

Christiano, T., 1996. *The rule of the many*. Boulder, Colo.: Westview Press.

Cohen, G.A., 1989. On the currency of egalitarian justice. *Ethics*, 99, 906–944.

Cohen, G.A., 2008. *Rescuing justice and equality*. Cambridge Mass.: Harvard University Press.

Goodin, R.E., 1981. The political theories of choice and dignity. *American philosophical quarterly*, 18 (2), 91–100.

Heath, J., 1997. Immigration, multiculturalism and the social contract. *Canadian journal of law and jurisprudence*, 10 (2), 343–361.

Hirschman, A.O., 1970. *Exit, voice and loyalty: responses to decline in firms, organizations and states*. Cambridge Mass.: Harvard University Press.

Mann, M., 2005. *The dark side of democracy: explaining ethnic cleansing*. Cambridge: Cambridge University Press.

Miller, D., 2007. *National responsibility and global justice*. Oxford: Oxford University Press.

Nagel, T., 2005. The problem of global justice. *Philosophy and public affairs*, 33, 113–147.

Neal, A.W., 2009. Securitization and risk at the EU border: the origins of FRONTEX*. *Journal of common market studies*, 47 (2), 333–356.

Parfit, D., 2000. Equality or priority? *In*: Matthew Clayton and Andrew Williams, eds. *The ideal of equality*. Basingstoke: Macmillan, 81–125.

Perry, St R., 1995. Immigration, justice, and culture. *In*: Warren F. Schwartz, ed. *Justice in immigration*. Cambridge: Cambridge University Press, 94–135.

Rawls, J., 1999a. *The law of peoples*. Cambridge, Mass.: Harvard University Press.

Rawls, J., 1999b. *A theory of justice*. 2nd ed. Cambridge, Mass.: Belknap Harvard.

Sen, A., 1999. *Development as freedom*. Oxford: Oxford University Press.

Shachar, A., 2009. *The birthright lottery: citizenship and global inequality*. Cambridge, Mass.: Harvard University Press.

Steiner, H., 2001. Hard borders, compensation, and classical liberalism. *In*: David Miller and Sohail H. Hashimi, eds. *Boundaries and justice: diverse ethical perspectives*. Princeton University Press: Princeton, 79–88.

Wellman, C.H., 2008. Immigration and the right to exclude. *Ethics*, 119, 109–141.

Index

Page numbers in *italic* type refer to *tables*
Page numbers followed by 'n' refer to notes